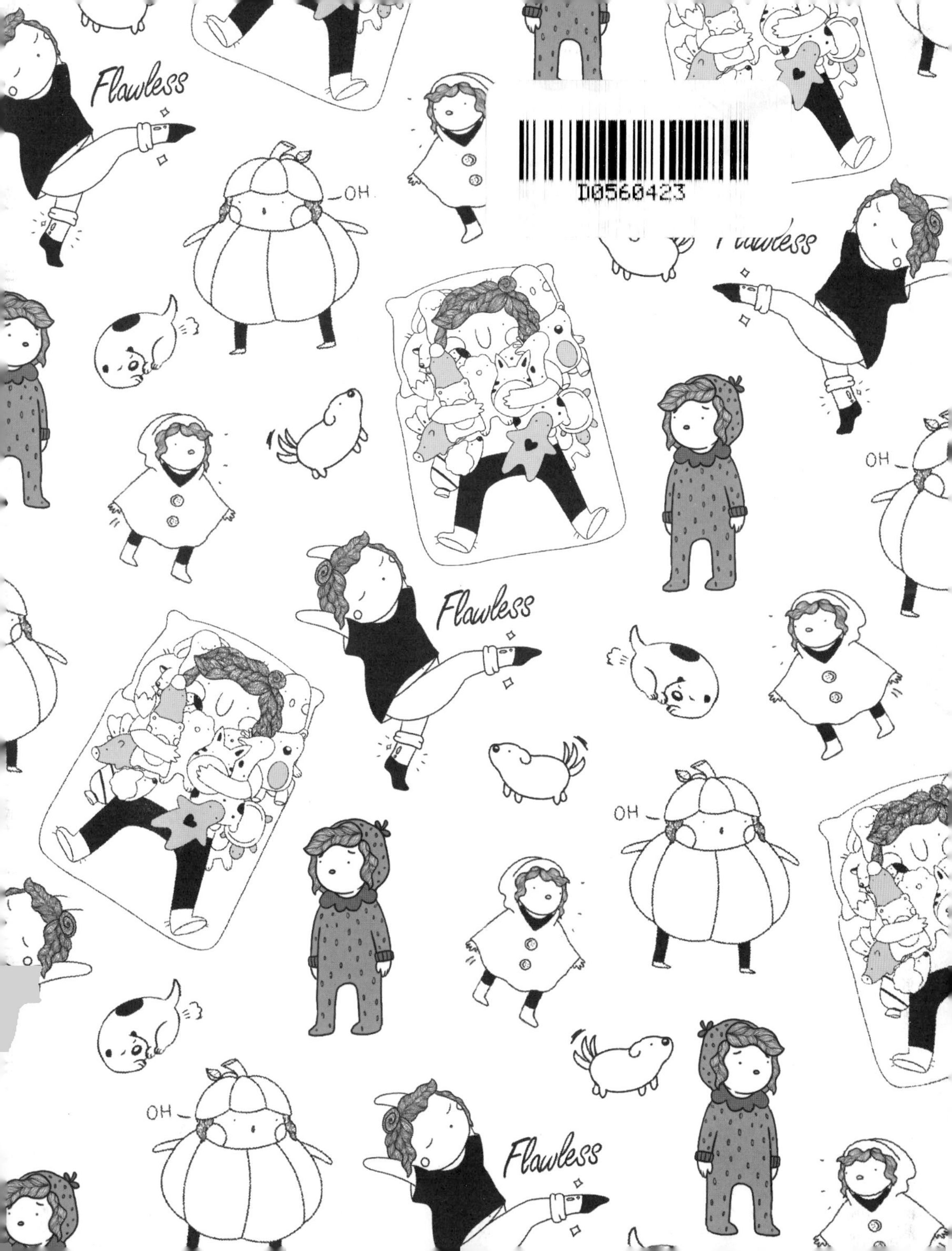
Flawless
OH
Flawless
OH
Flawless
OH
OH
Flawless

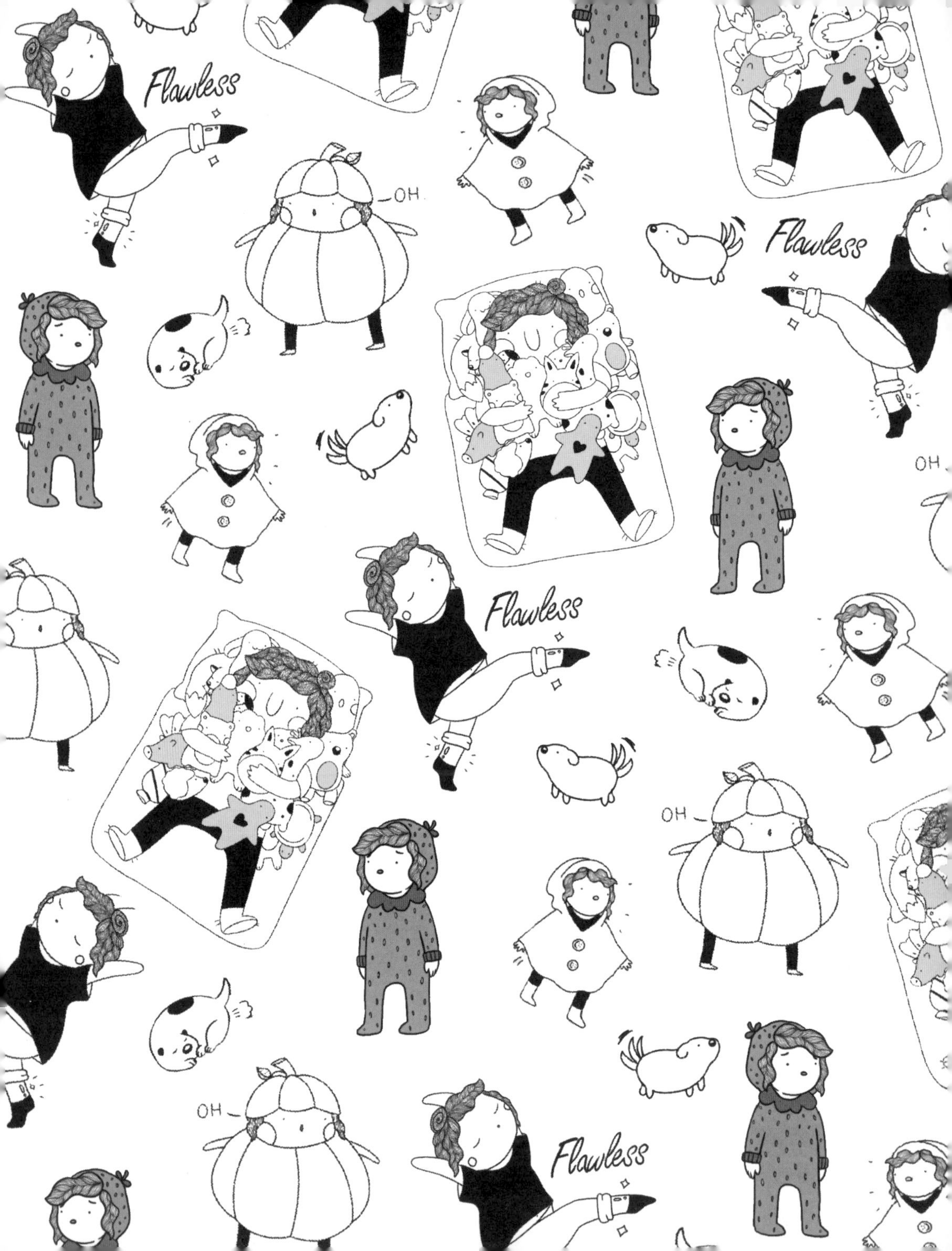
Flawless
OH
Flawless
OH
Flawless
OH
OH
Flawless

small hours

A MRS. FROLLEIN COLLECTION

VALÉRIE MINELLI

Published by Oni-Lion Forge Publishing Group, LLC

Designed by Leigh Luna
Edited by Jasmine Amiri

James Lucas Jones, president & publisher
Sarah Gaydos, editor in chief
Charlie Chu, e.v.p. of creative & business development
Brad Rooks, director of operations
Amber O'Neill, special projects manager
Harris Fish, events manager
Margot Wood, director of marketing & sales
Jeremy Atkins, director of brand communications
Devin Funches, sales & marketing manager
Tara Lehmann, marketing & publicity associate
Troy Look, director of design & production
Kate Z. Stone, senior graphic designer
Sonja Synak, graphic designer
Hilary Thompson, graphic designer

Angie Knowles, digital prepress lead
Shawna Gore, senior editor
Robin Herrera, senior editor
Amanda Meadows, senior editor
Jasmine Amiri, senior editor
Grace Bornhoft, editor
Zack Soto, editor
Steve Ellis, director of games
Ben Eisner, game developer
Michelle Nguyen, executive assistant
Jung Lee, logistics coordinator

Joe Nozemack, publisher emeritus

onipress.com | lionforge.com
facebook.com/onipress | facebook.com/lionforge
twitter.com/onipress | twitter.com/lionforge
instagram.com/onipress | instagram.com/lionforge
instagram.com/mrs.frollein
mrsfrollein.com

First Edition: February 2020

ISBN 978-1-62010-715-7

eISBN 978-1-62010-724-9

Printed in China

Library of Congress Control Number: 2019945815

2 3 4 5 6 7 8 9 10

FOREWORD—

There is a formula in comedic webcomics that has dominated the medium for many years. We call it #sadbutfunny — a four-panel strip that ends on a cynical note. For a long time, we were amazed by this detached tone and loved the hopeless characters that helped us ease the pain of our own bittersweet self-pity. But then, something changed.

The thing is: A joke is only funny if there's a certain amount of distance between you and its protagonists, especially when it comes to sad punchlines. Due to a few specific world leaders and movements, our environment appears more sad and more bitter than it used to. What we need is something to give us hope.

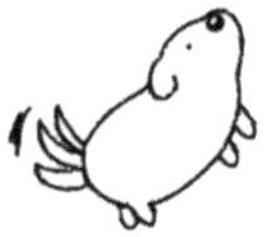

This is where Valérie Minelli enters the game and sweeps us off our sad little feet with her heartwarming world. Her comics are wholesome stories of candid everyday life. Of having a crush and hoping that someone will love us back, of pursuing our dreams, of actually caring about things and not being afraid or too cool to show it. The time for genuine heartfelt comics has arrived and Minelli is one of its funniest voices. When the world seems to fall apart, this book has the strength to put it back together.

Jonathan Kunz & Elizabeth Pich
War and Peas

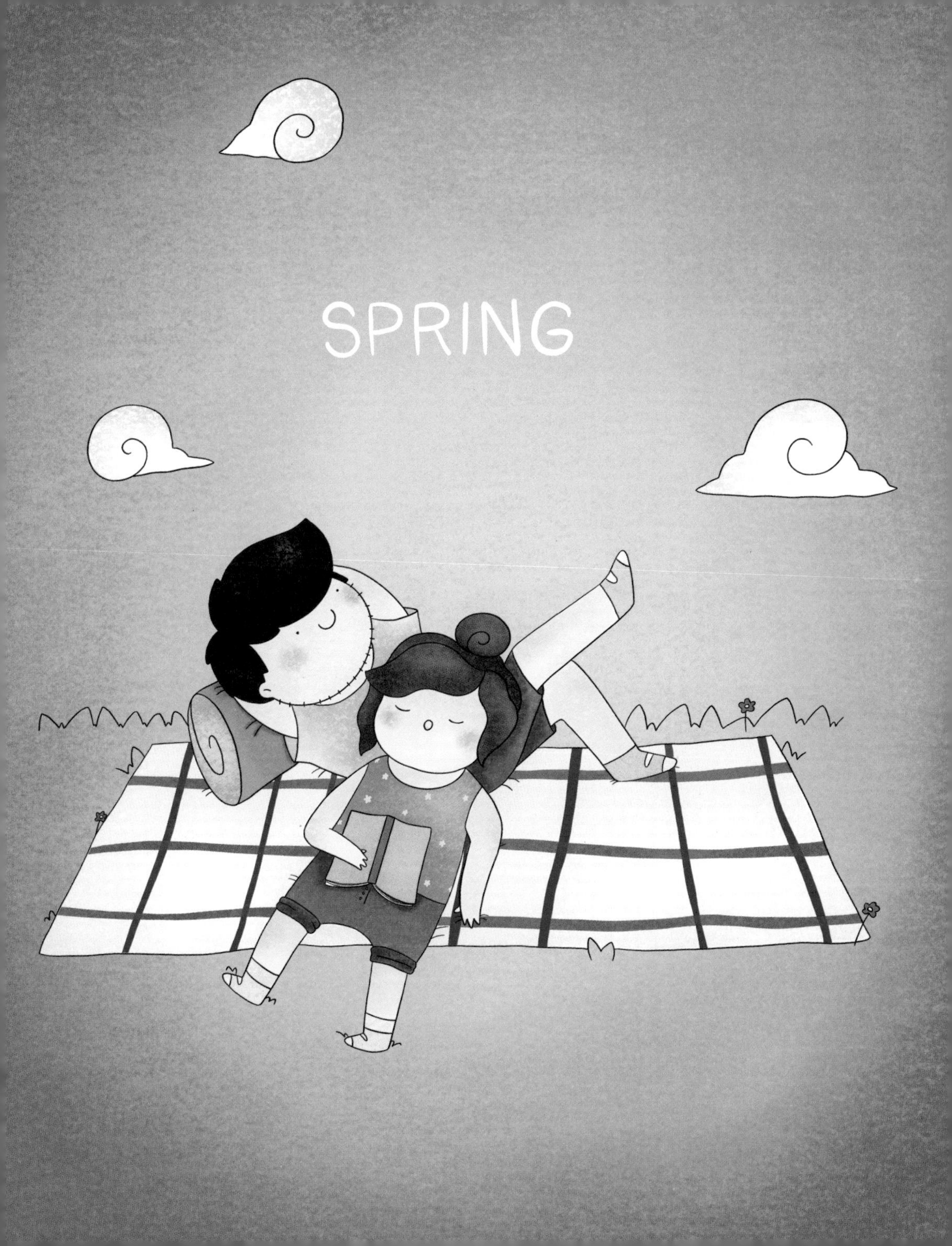
SPRING

NEW FLAT

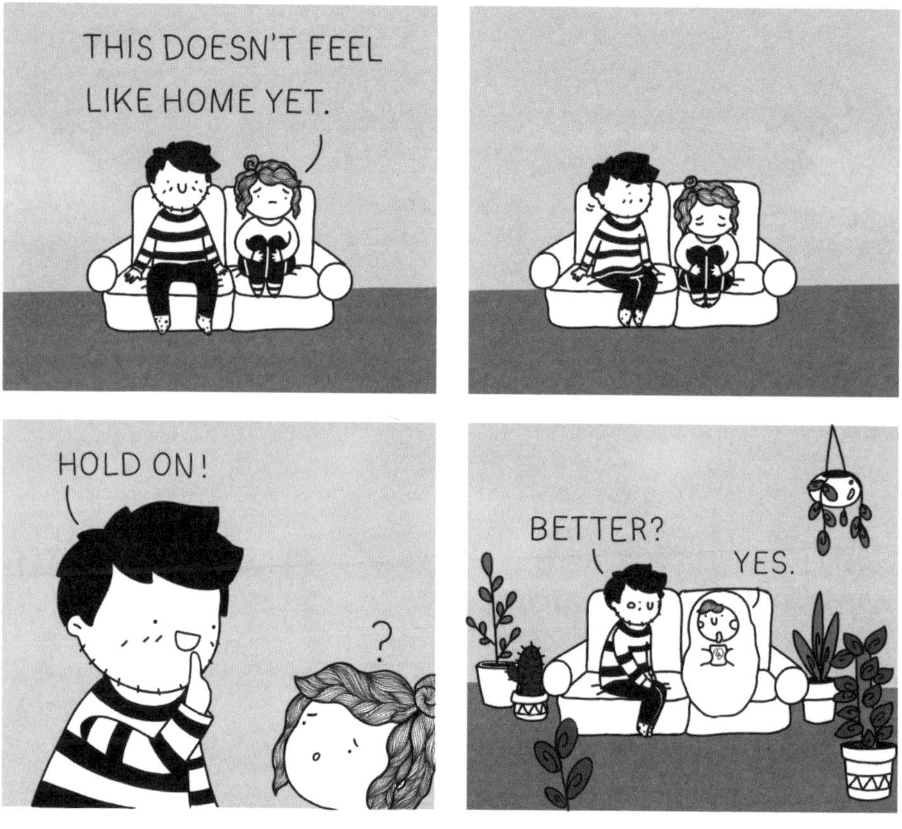
THIS DOESN'T FEEL LIKE HOME YET.
HOLD ON!
?
BETTER?
YES.

MORNING BREATH

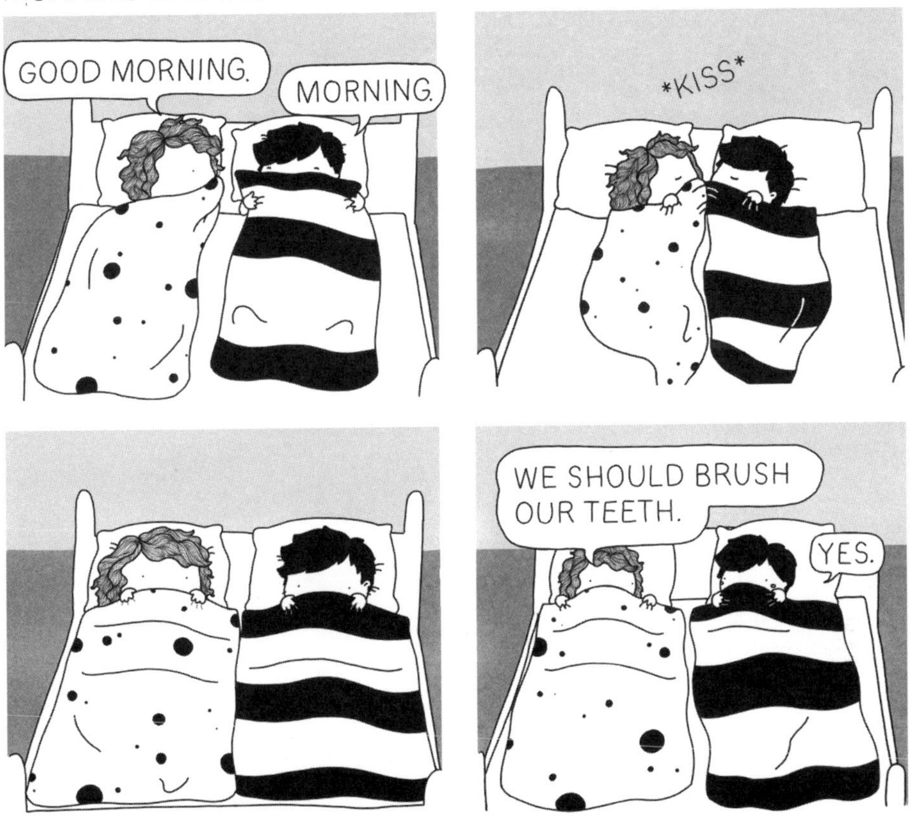
GOOD MORNING.
MORNING.
KISS
WE SHOULD BRUSH OUR TEETH.
YES.

BEAUTY BLOGGER

DONE! FINALLY!
CAN'T DO IT. TOO SHY.
NOPE.
WIPE

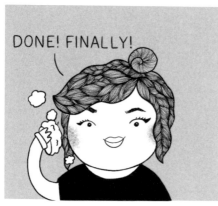

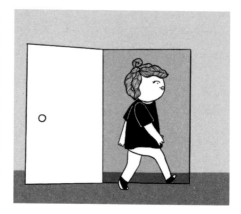

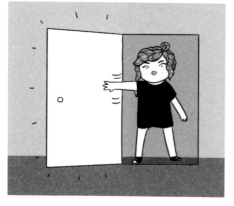

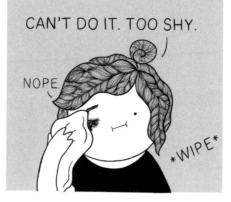

YOU MAY ALSO LIKE

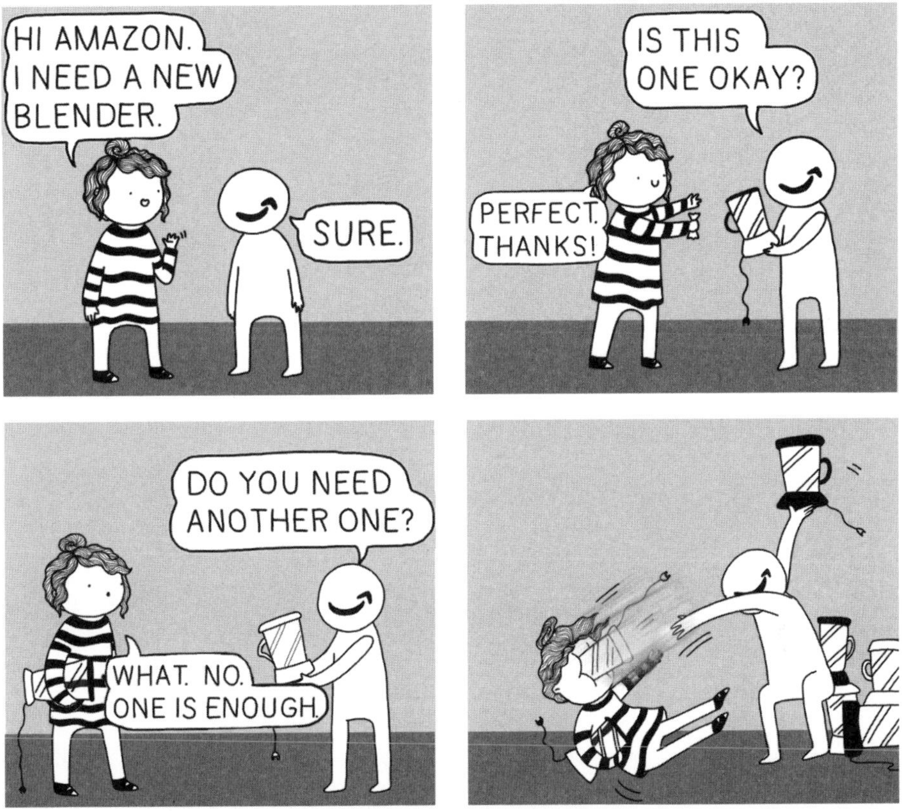
HI AMAZON. I NEED A NEW BLENDER.
SURE.
IS THIS ONE OKAY?
PERFECT. THANKS!
DO YOU NEED ANOTHER ONE?
WHAT. NO. ONE IS ENOUGH.

LONG-DISTANCE RELATIONSHIP

HI MOM!
UH-HUH.
BLABLA
HI! I'M TALKING TO YOUR SISTER. DO YOU WANT TO SAY HELLO?
YES!
YOU'RE A BIG OLD FART!
HAHAHA!
HAHAHA!

TEAM

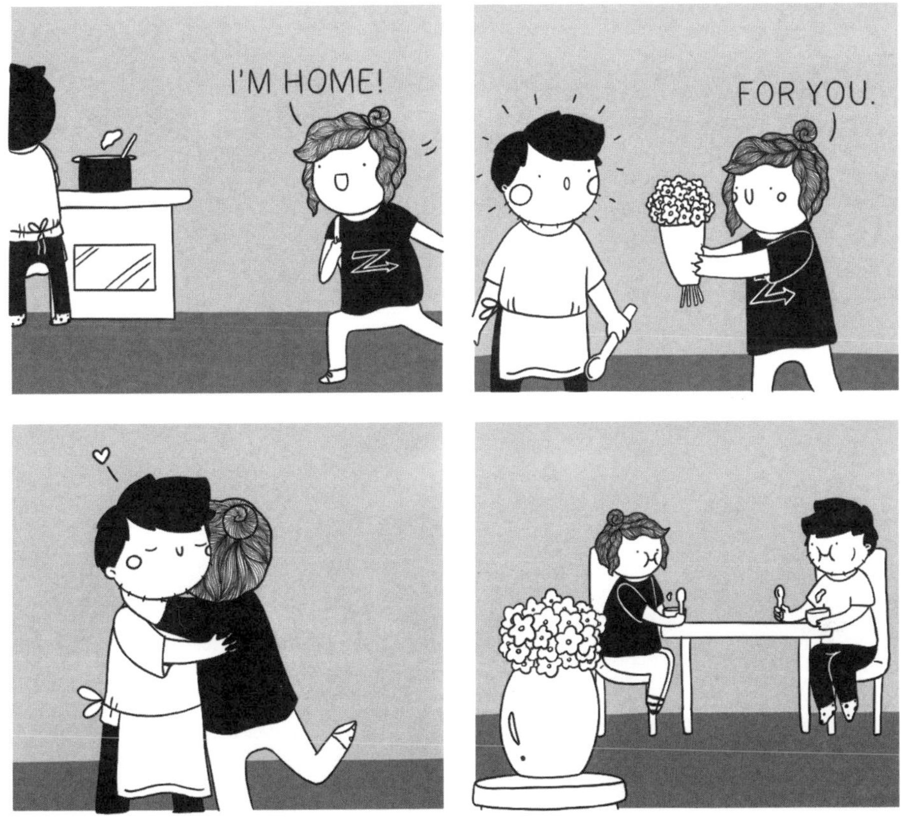
I'M HOME!
FOR YOU.

CHANGES

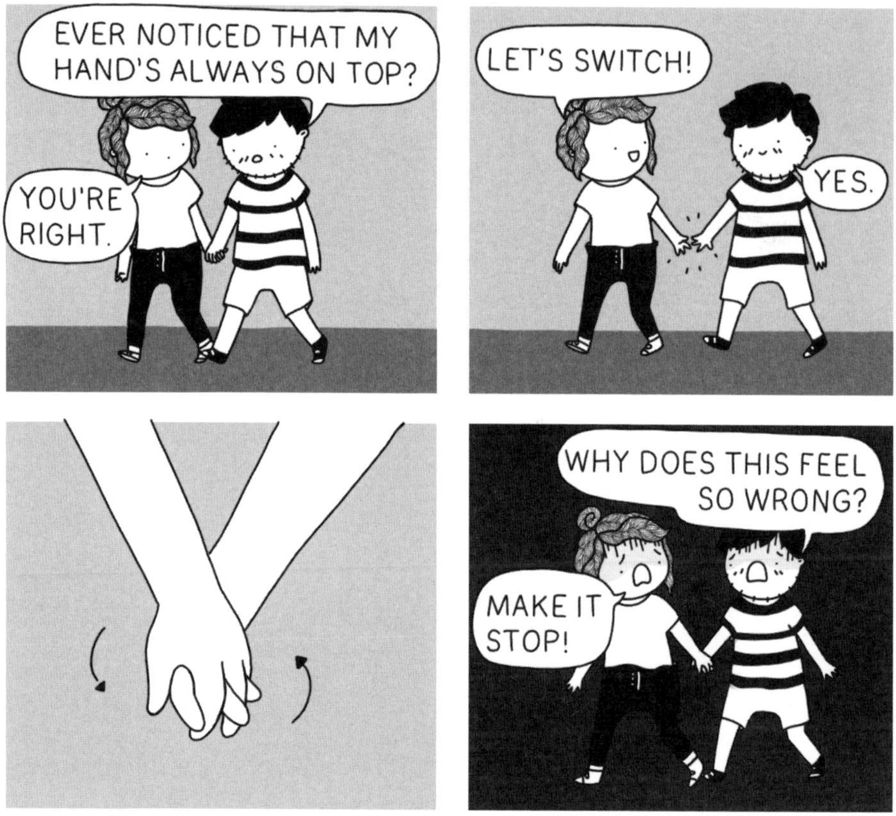
EVER NOTICED THAT MY HAND'S ALWAYS ON TOP?
YOU'RE RIGHT.
LET'S SWITCH!
YES.
WHY DOES THIS FEEL SO WRONG?
MAKE IT STOP!

HAWK-EYED

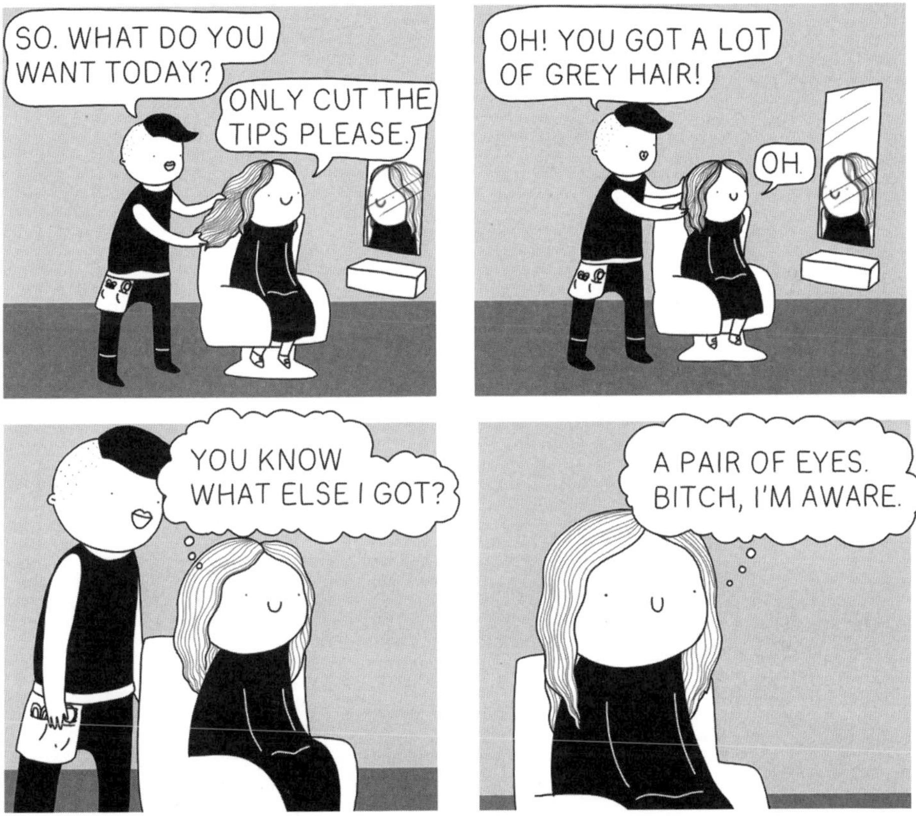
SO. WHAT DO YOU WANT TODAY?
ONLY CUT THE TIPS PLEASE.
OH! YOU GOT A LOT OF GREY HAIR!
OH.
YOU KNOW WHAT ELSE I GOT?
A PAIR OF EYES. BITCH, I'M AWARE.

ROADTRIP

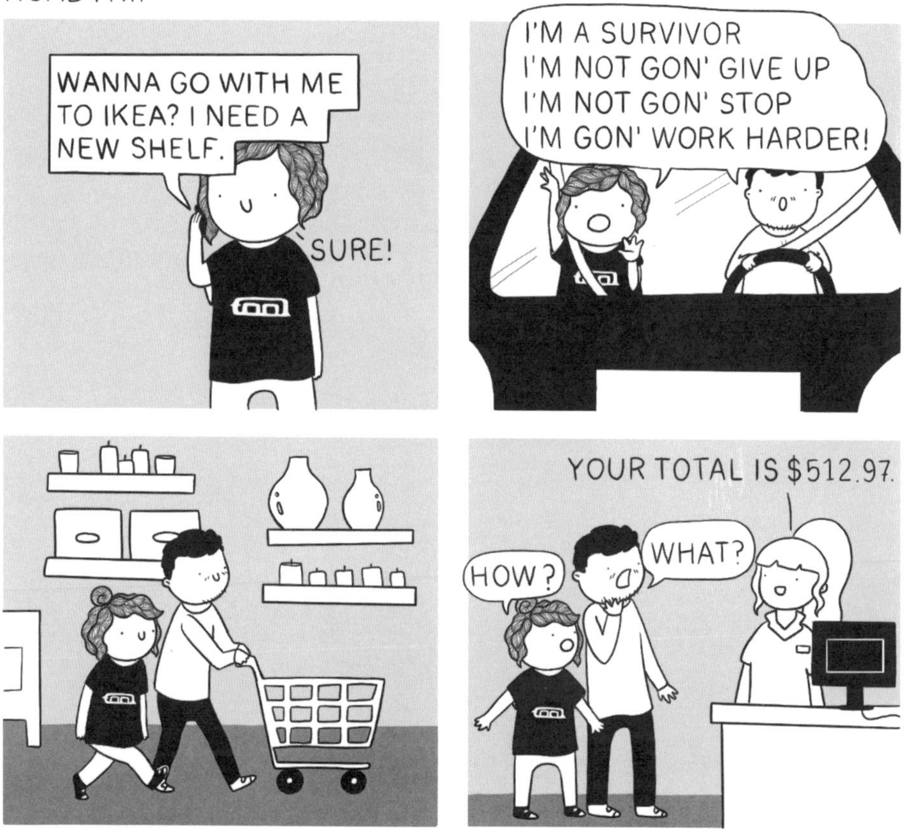
WANNA GO WITH ME TO IKEA? I NEED A NEW SHELF.
SURE!
I'M A SURVIVOR
I'M NOT GON' GIVE UP
I'M NOT GON' STOP
I'M GON' WORK HARDER!
YOUR TOTAL IS $512.97.
HOW?
WHAT?

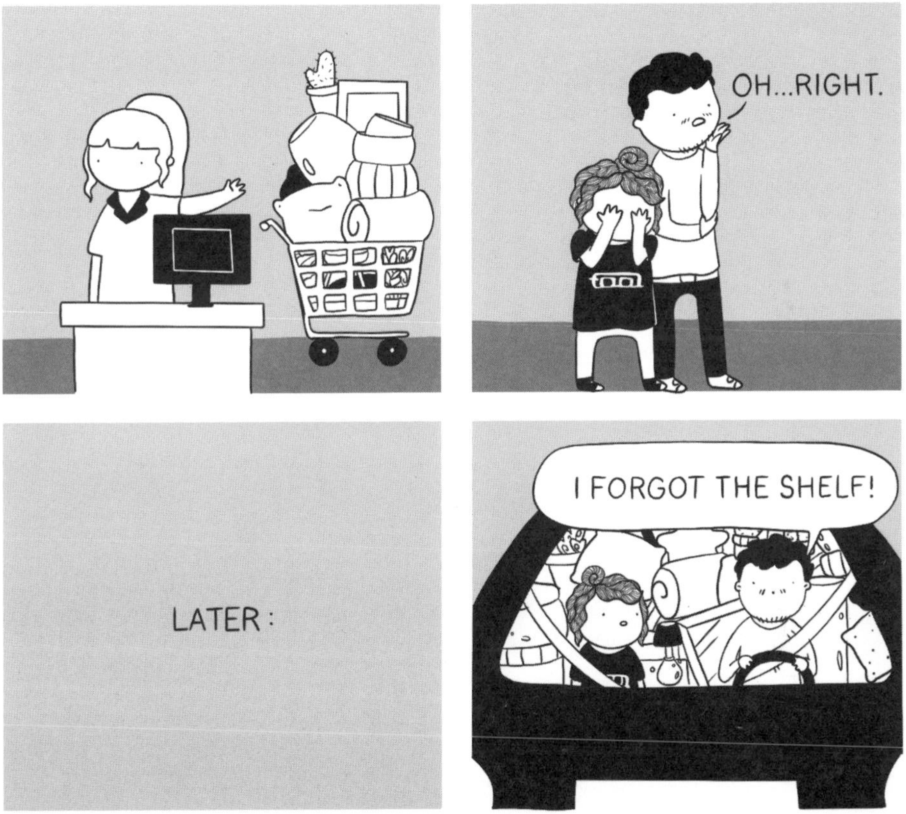
OH...RIGHT.
LATER:
I FORGOT THE SHELF!

SO CUTE

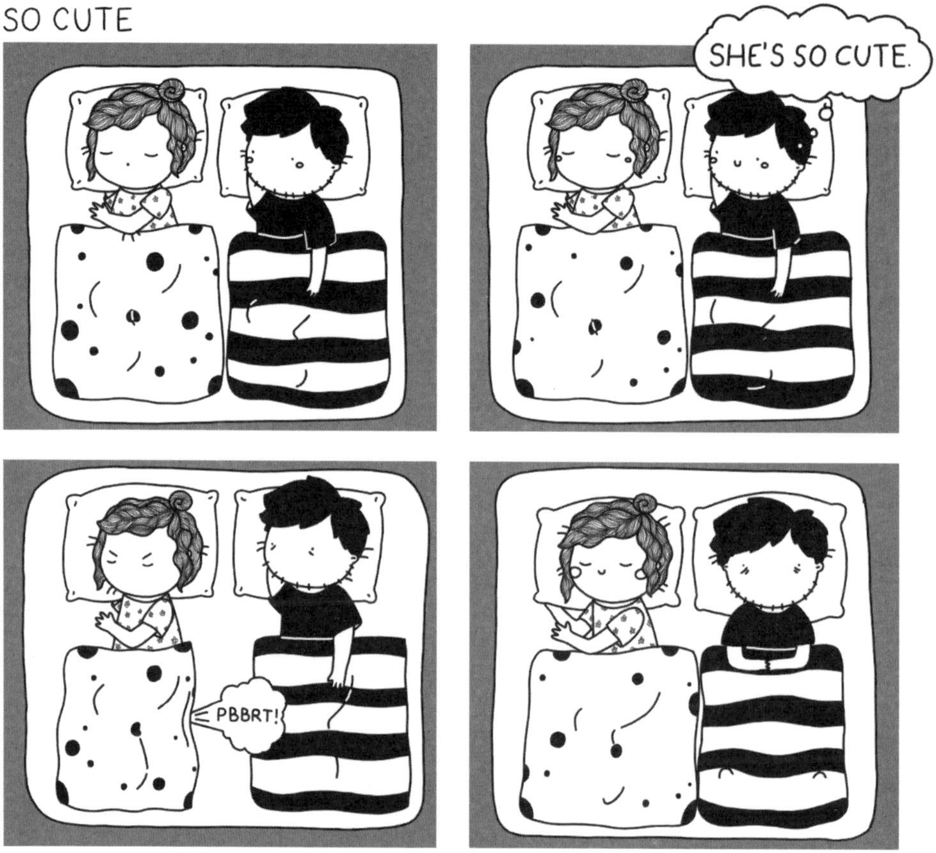
SHE'S SO CUTE.
PBBRT!

WHEN YOUR FAVORITE SONG COMES ON

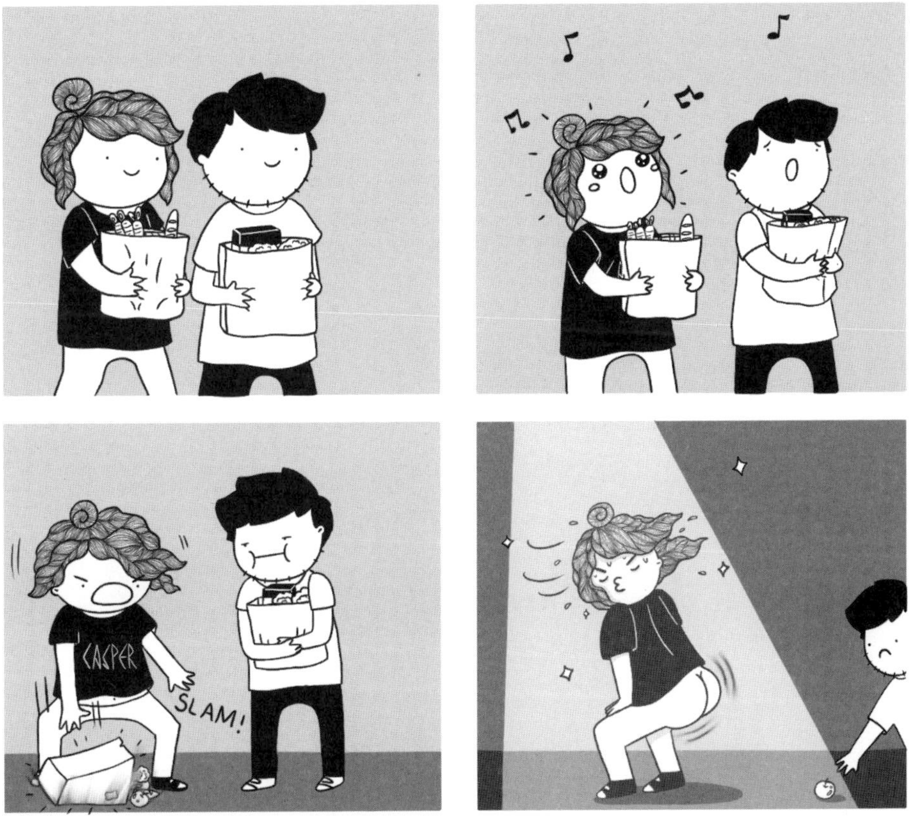
CASPER
SLAM!

FIRST TATTOO

I GOT "ONE STEP CLOSER" ON MY FOOT, SO I WILL ALWAYS REMEMBER THAT EVERY STEP IS A STEP CLOSER TO MY GOAL.

I THOUGHT ABOUT IT FOR A LONG TIME AND WANTED TO KEEP IT SMALL AND SIMPLE.

7TH TATTOO

I DON'T KNOW... I LIKE CROISSANTS.

MEATBALLS

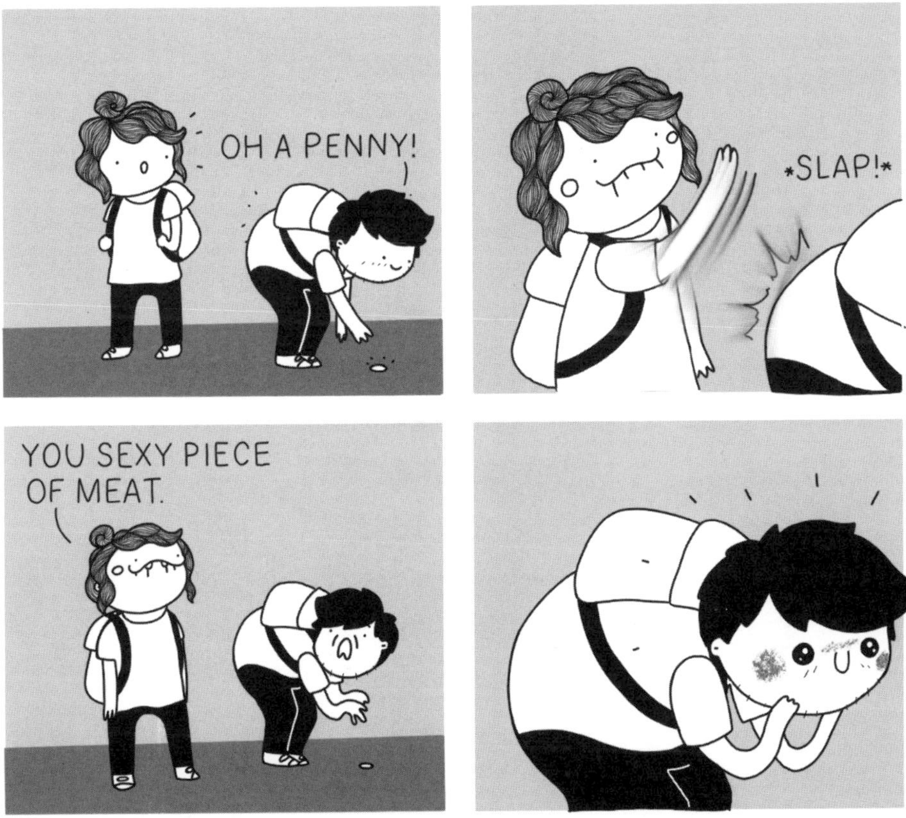
OH A PENNY!
SLAP!
YOU SEXY PIECE OF MEAT.

WE FIGHT BUT STILL HOLD TIGHT

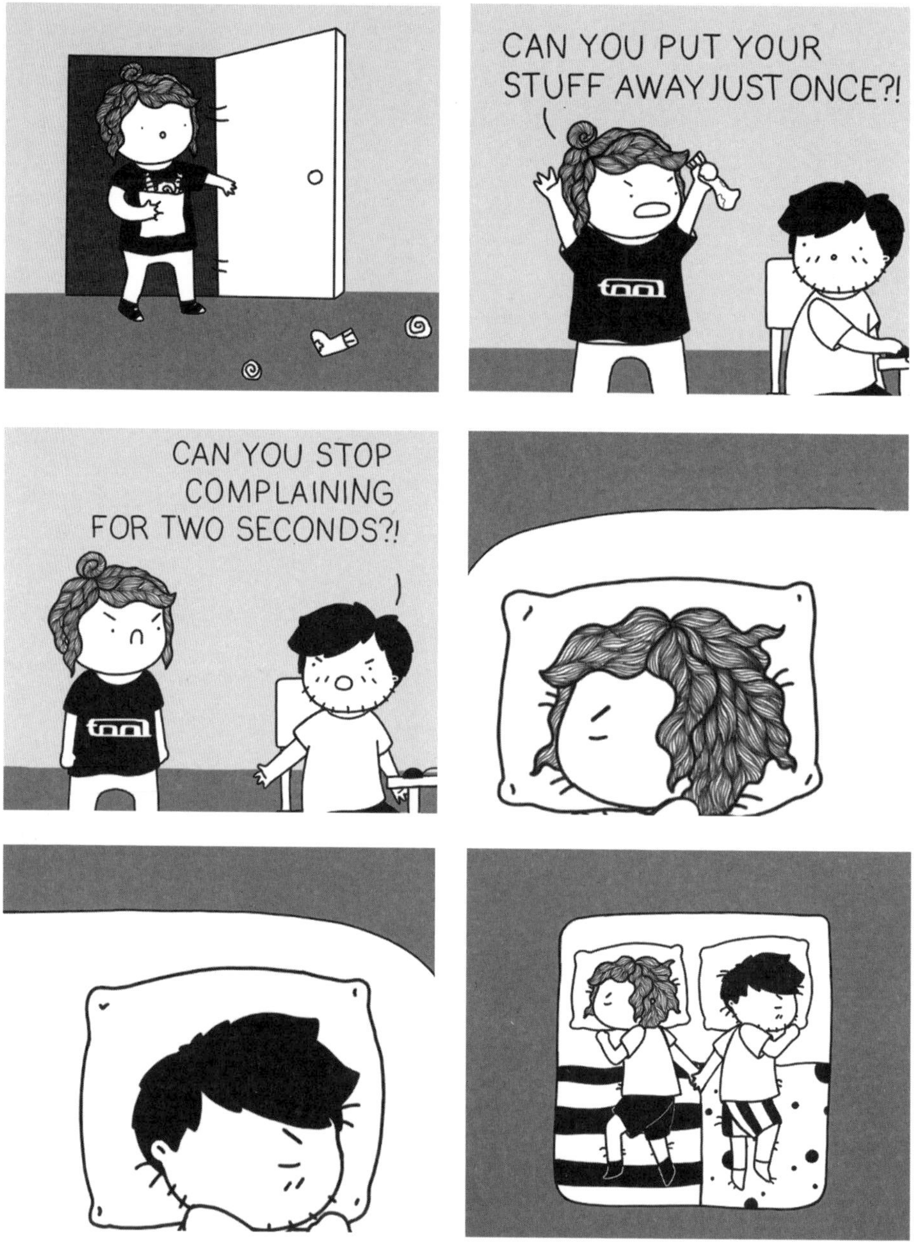
CAN YOU PUT YOUR STUFF AWAY JUST ONCE?!
CAN YOU STOP COMPLAINING FOR TWO SECONDS?!

PRINCE CHARMING

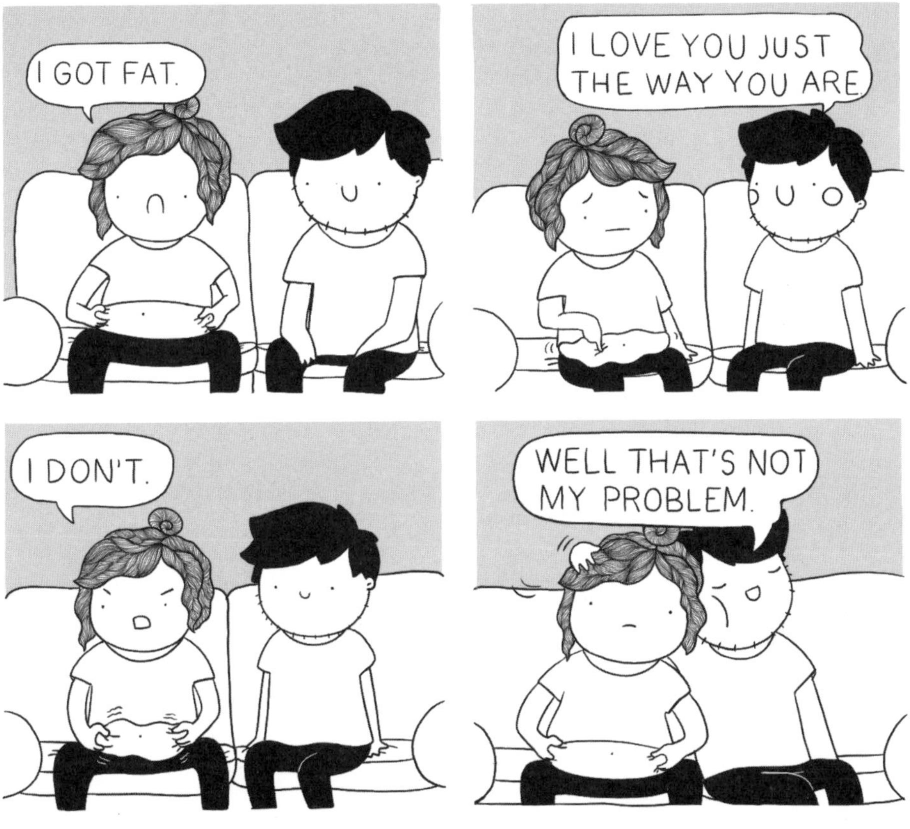
I GOT FAT.
I LOVE YOU JUST THE WAY YOU ARE.
I DON'T.
WELL THAT'S NOT MY PROBLEM.

PROGRESS

OH, SOME OF MY
OLD DRAWINGS.
OH MY...
GAWD.
MY DRAWING SKILLS
HAVE REALLY IMPROVED!

SUMMER

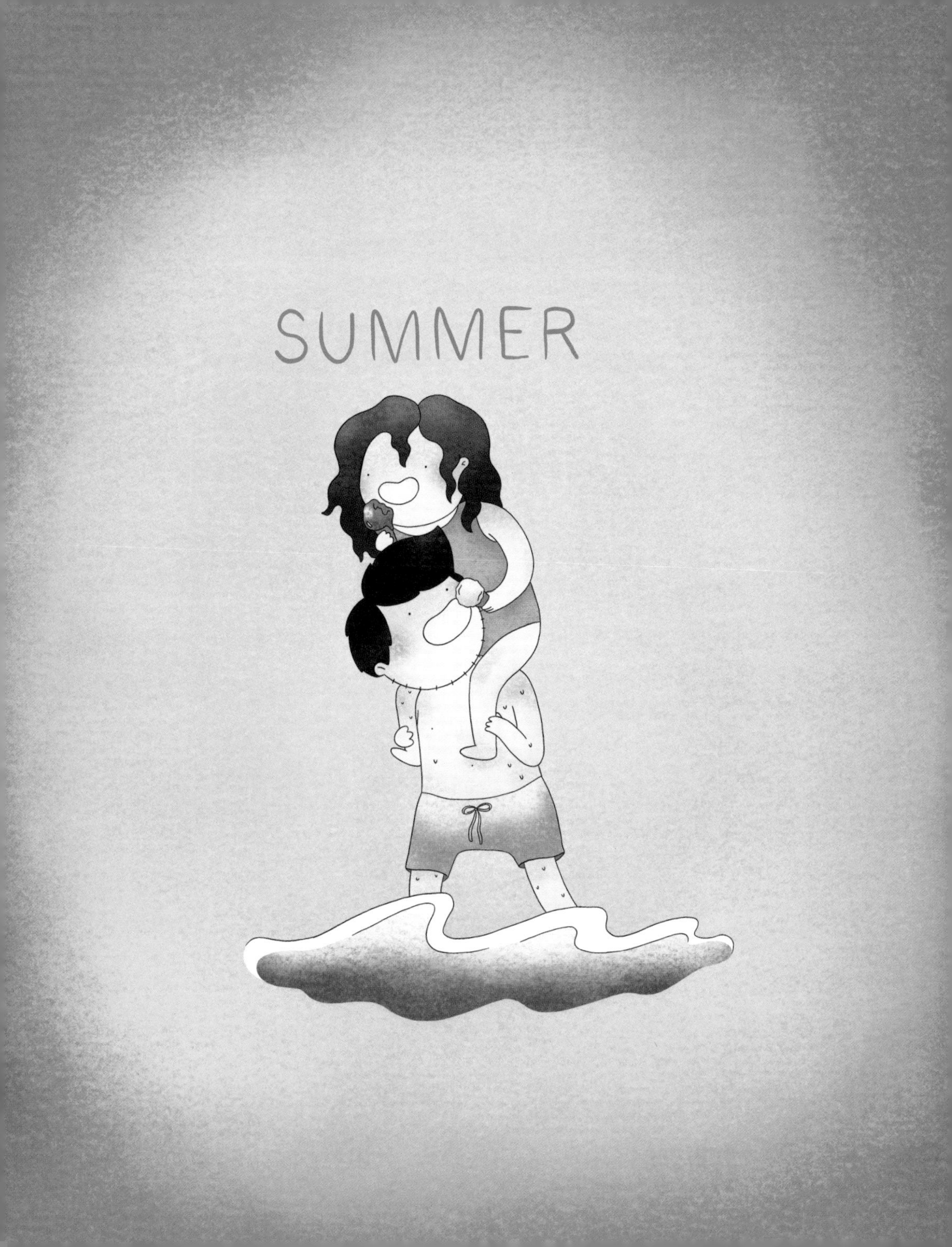

FINALLY

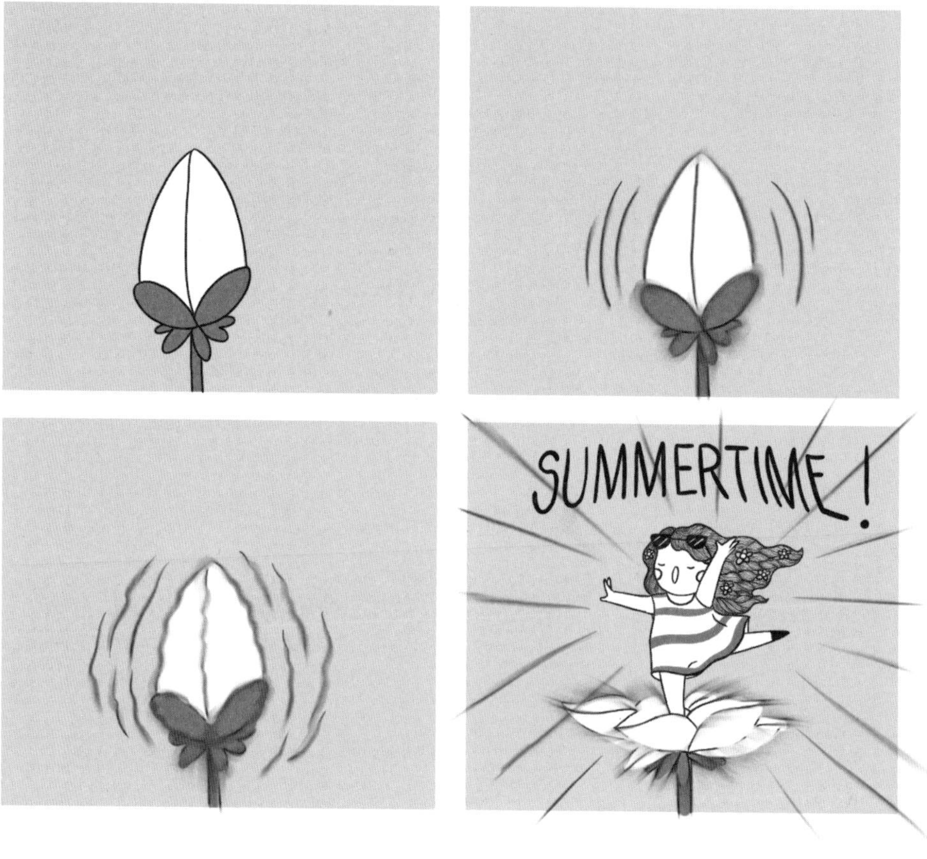
SUMMERTIME!

DRESS CODE

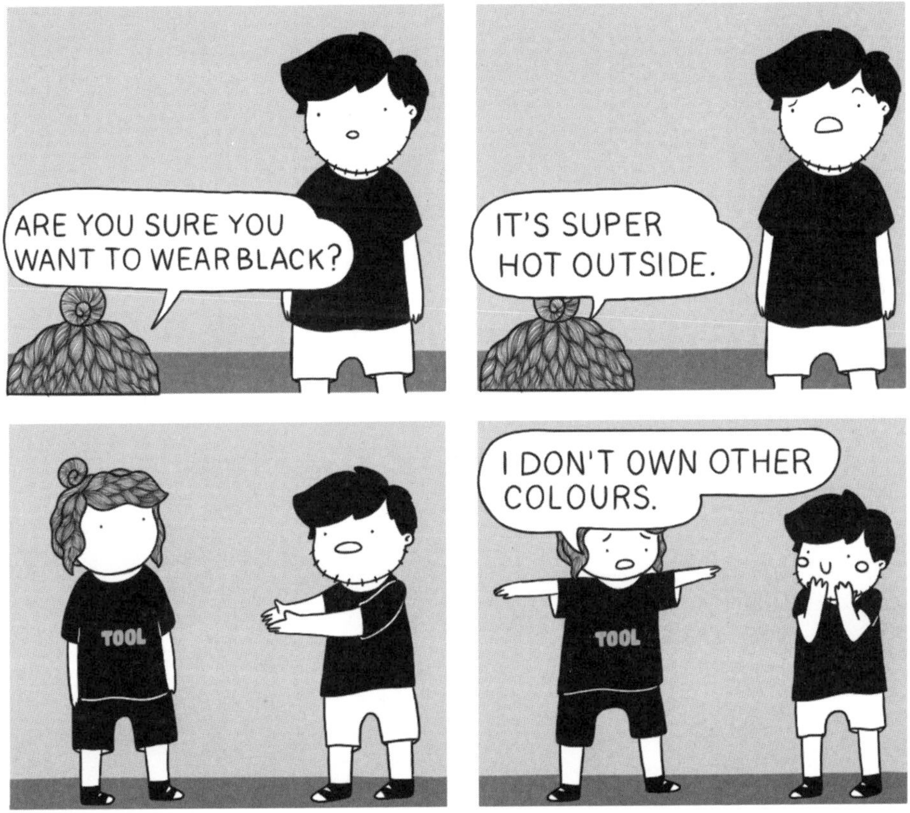
ARE YOU SURE YOU WANT TO WEAR BLACK?
IT'S SUPER HOT OUTSIDE.
TOOL
TOOL
I DON'T OWN OTHER COLOURS.

GUNS

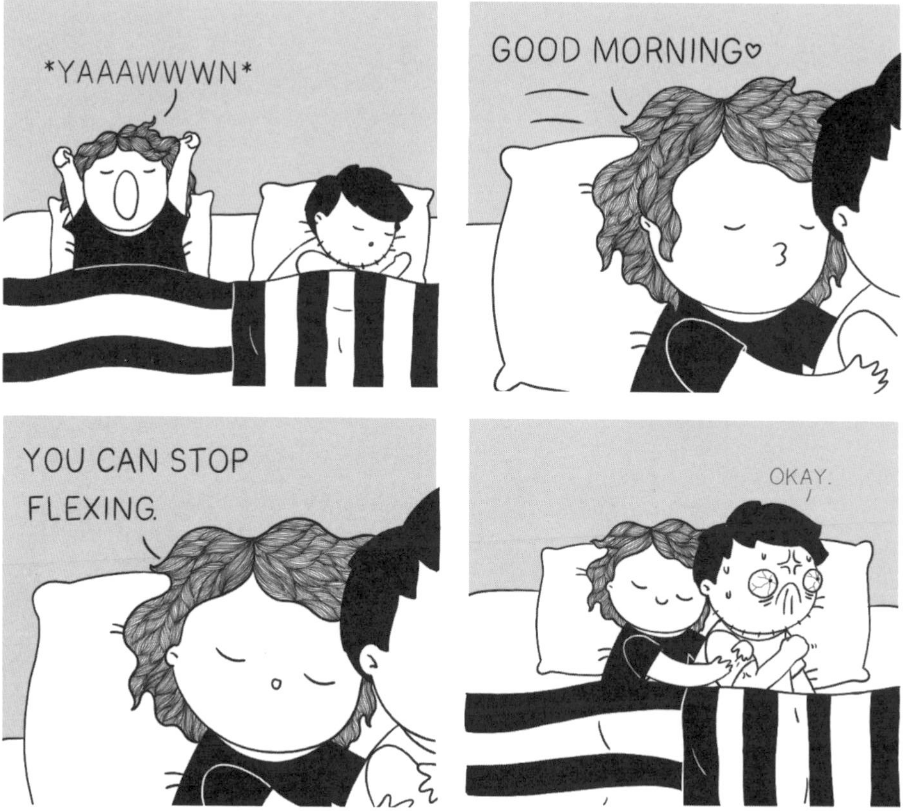
YAAAWWWN
GOOD MORNING♡
YOU CAN STOP FLEXING.
OKAY.

THAT'LL DO PIG

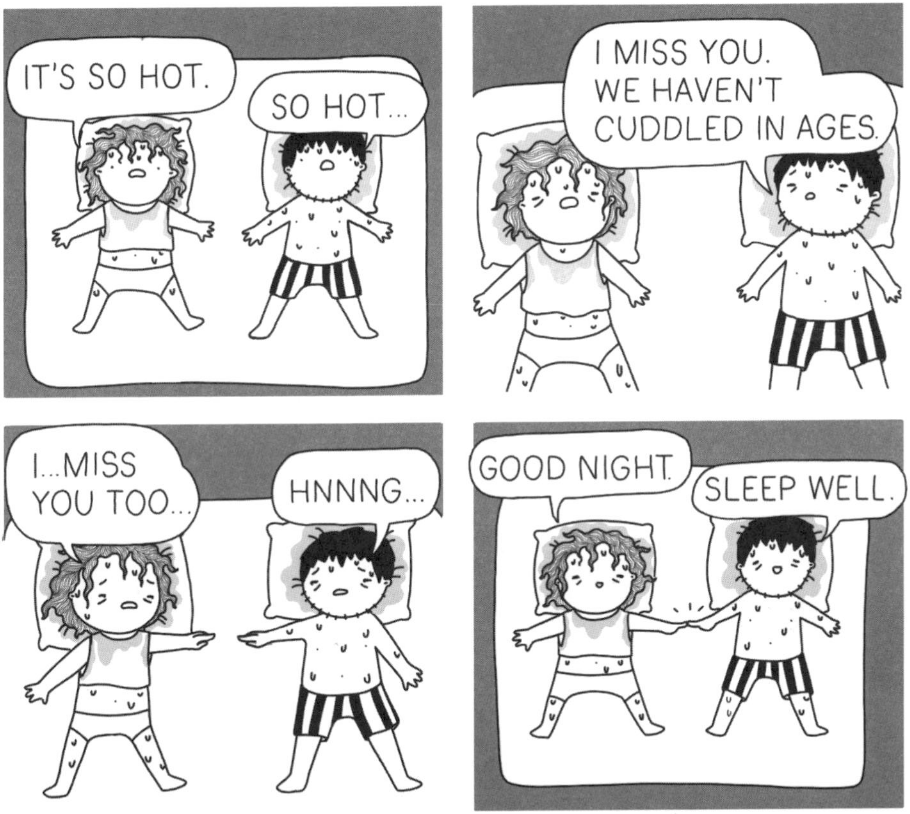
IT'S SO HOT.
SO HOT...
I MISS YOU. WE HAVEN'T CUDDLED IN AGES.
I...MISS YOU TOO...
HNNNG...
GOOD NIGHT.
SLEEP WELL.

DIFFERENCES

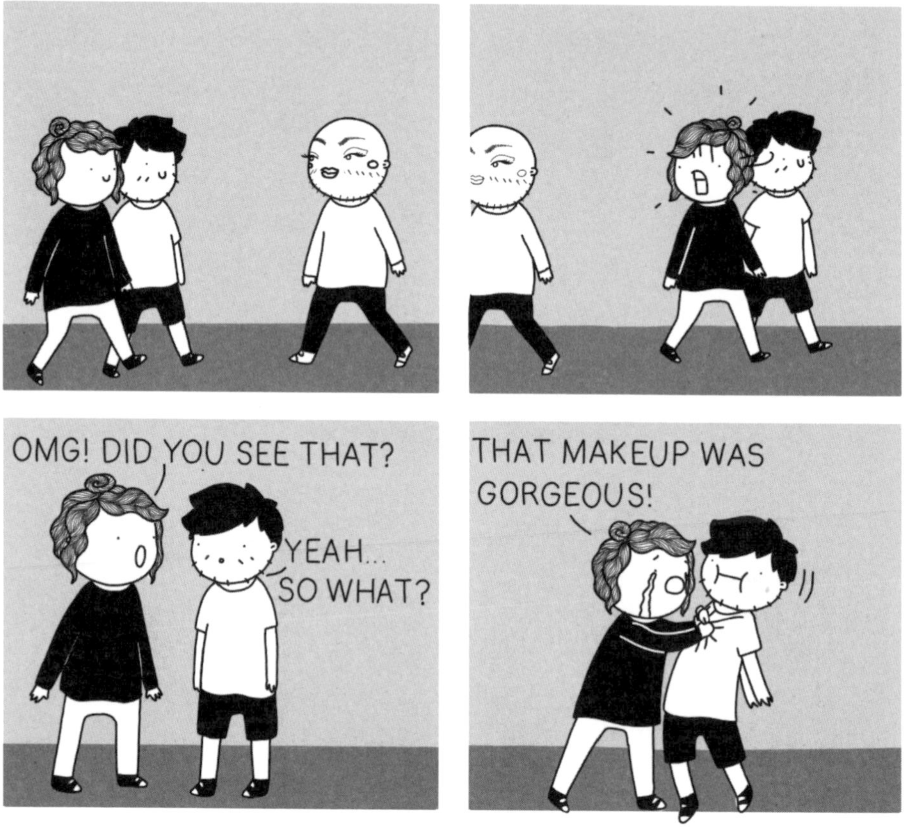

OMG! DID YOU SEE THAT?
YEAH... SO WHAT?
THAT MAKEUP WAS GORGEOUS!

BLOODY AWESOME

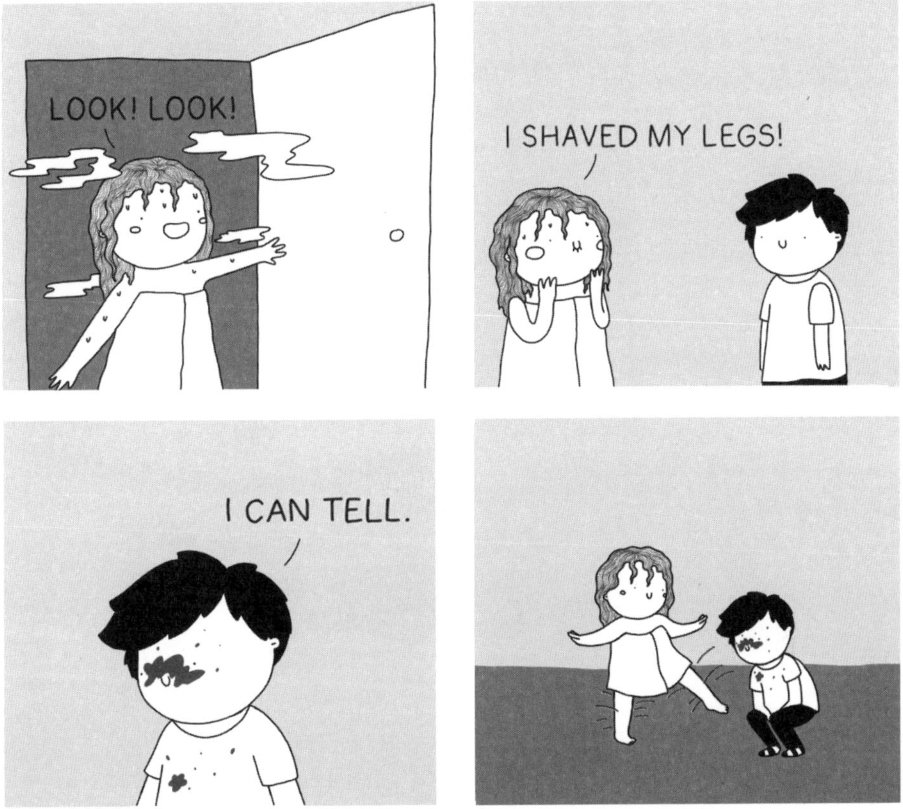
LOOK! LOOK!
I SHAVED MY LEGS!
I CAN TELL.

HOLY FROLLEIN

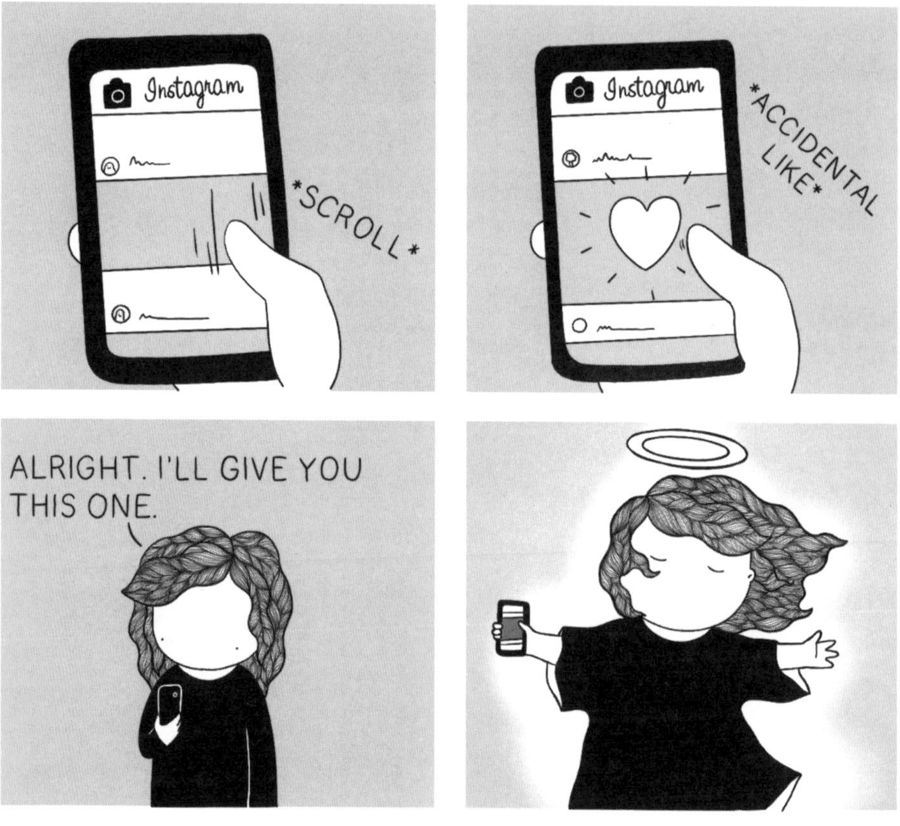
Instagram
SCROLL
Instagram
ACCIDENTAL LIKE
ALRIGHT. I'LL GIVE YOU THIS ONE.

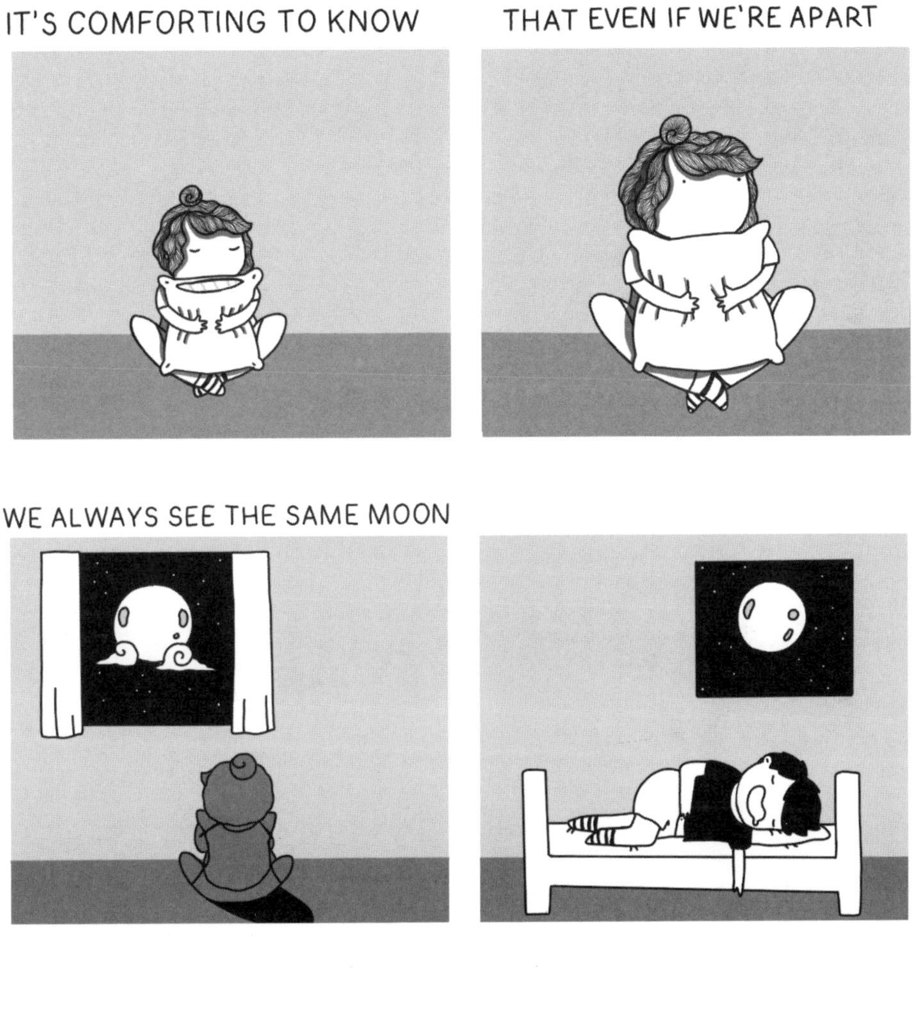
IT'S COMFORTING TO KNOW
THAT EVEN IF WE'RE APART
WE ALWAYS SEE THE SAME MOON

SUMMER LOVING

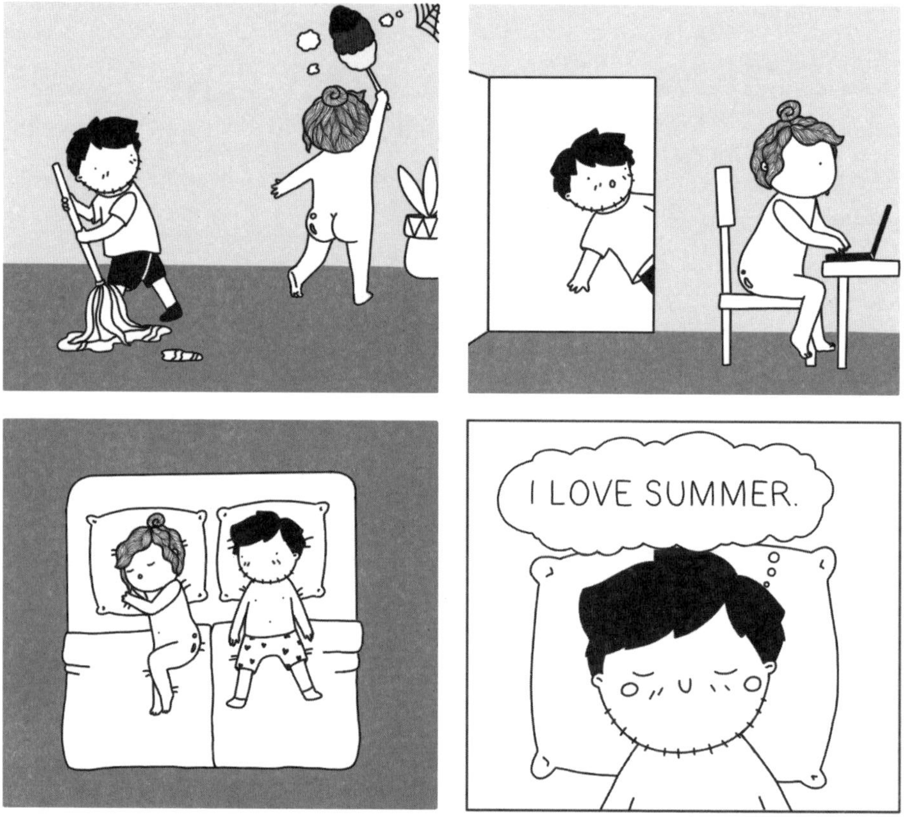
I LOVE SUMMER.

PRAGMATIC

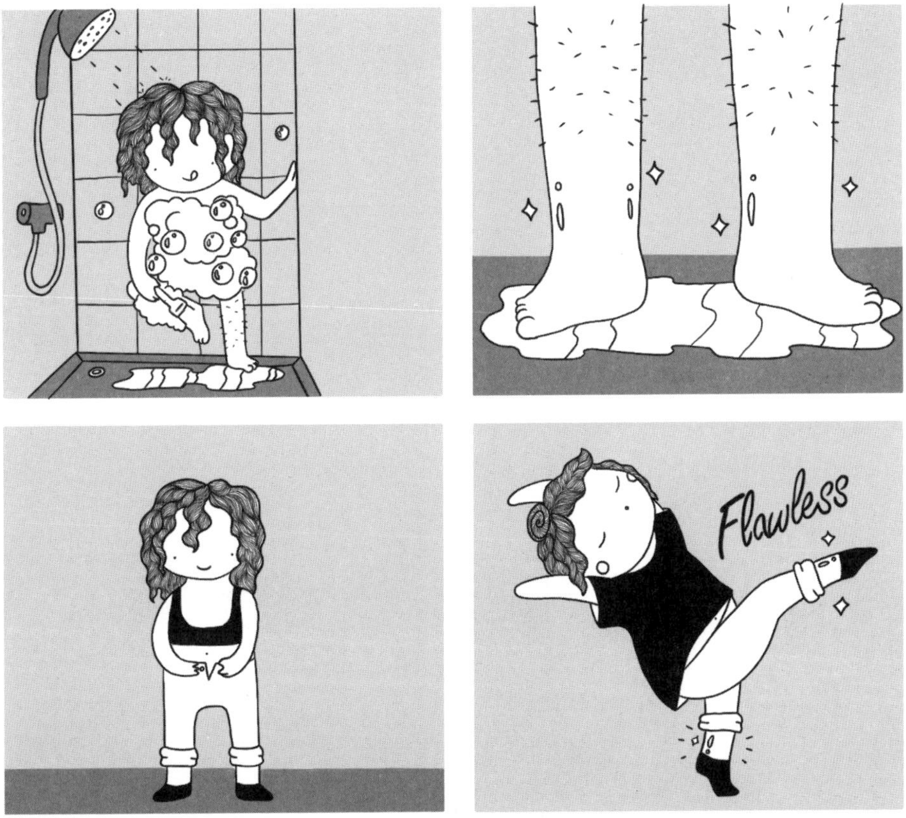
Flawless

TICKLE MONSTER

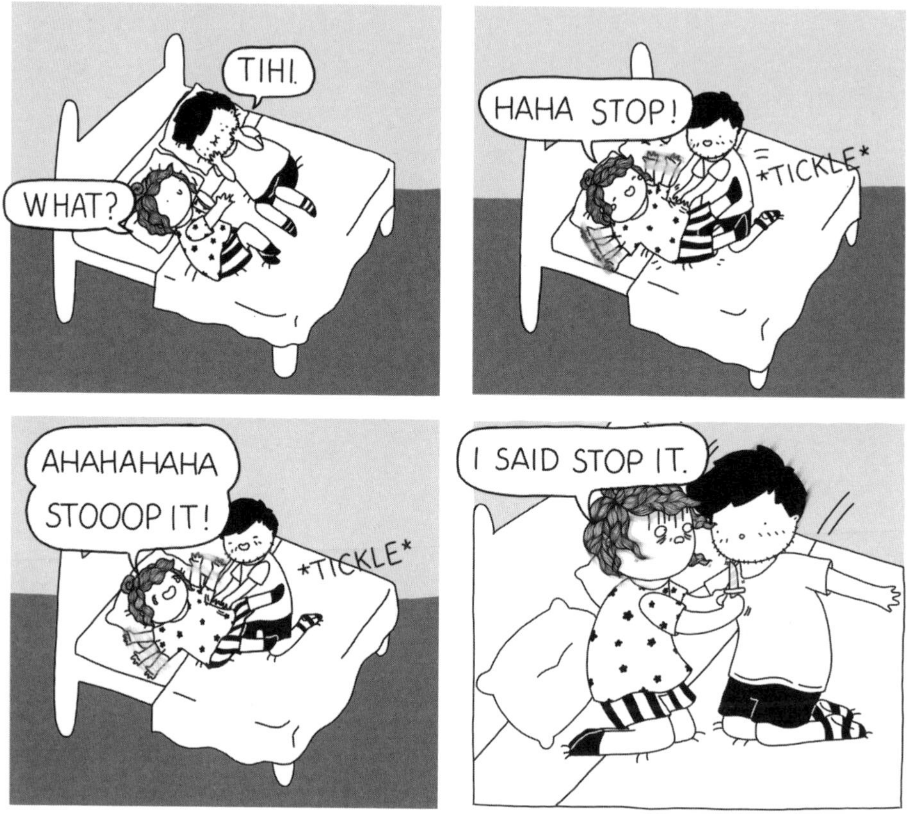
TIHI.
WHAT?
HAHA STOP!
TICKLE
AHAHAHAHA STOOOP IT!
TICKLE
I SAID STOP IT.

CREATURE OF HABIT

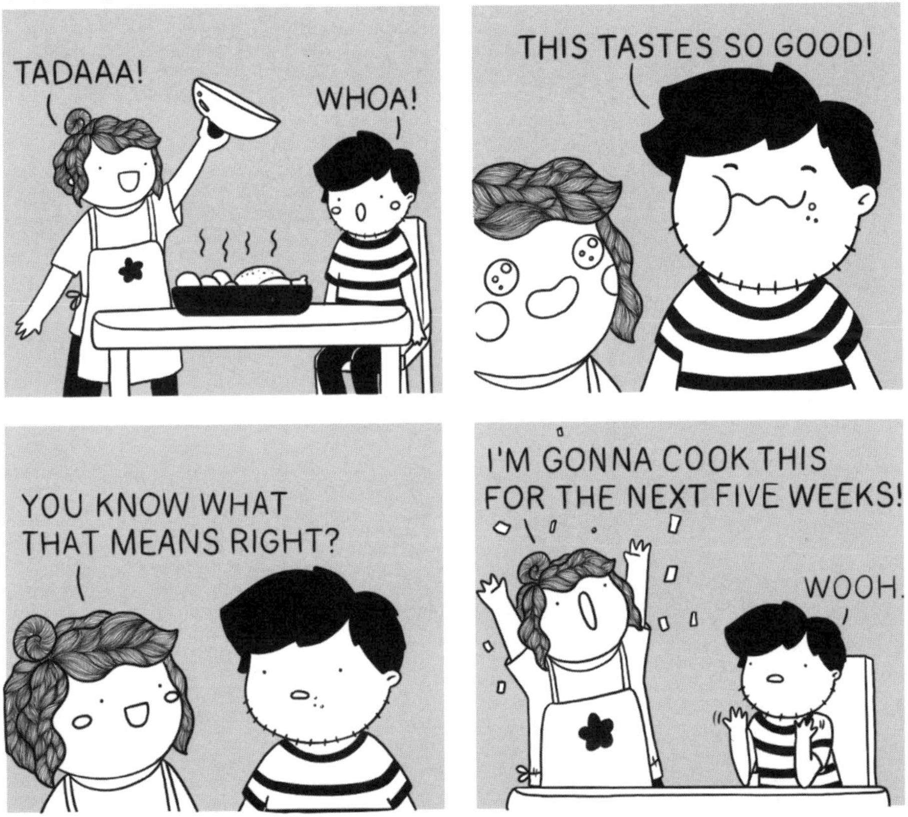
TADAAA!
WHOA!
THIS TASTES SO GOOD!
YOU KNOW WHAT THAT MEANS RIGHT?
I'M GONNA COOK THIS FOR THE NEXT FIVE WEEKS!
WOOH.

DESPERATE KINDNESS

ARE YOU HUNGRY?
NO.
SHALL I COOK SOMETHING?
BUT I'M NOT HUNG-
GIVE ME A CHANCE TO DO SOMETHING NICE, WOMAN!

THANK YOU

WHOA

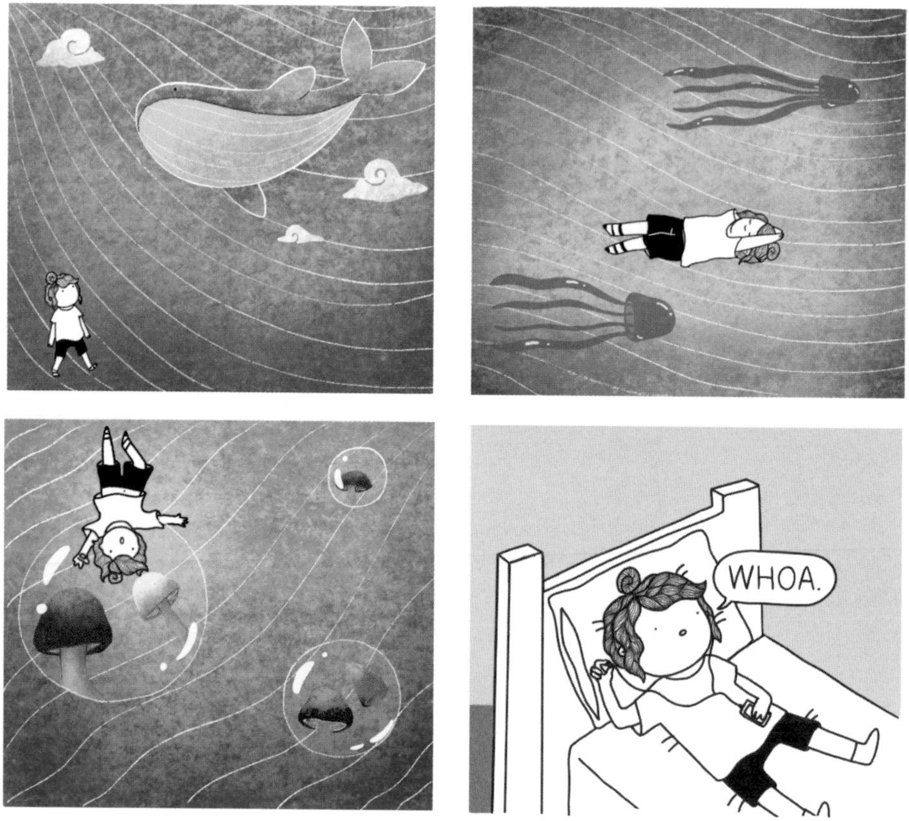
WHOA.

DON'T BLINK

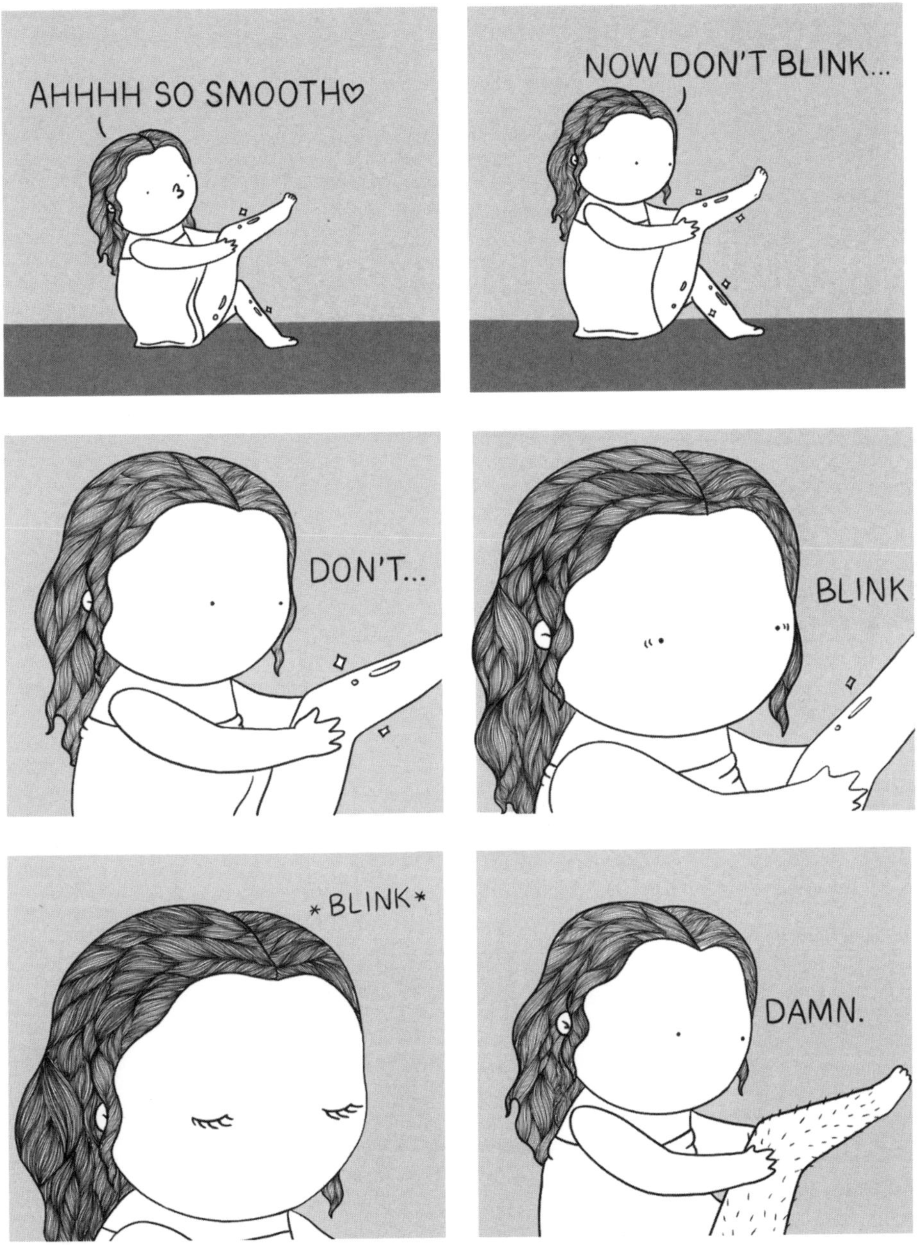
AHHHH SO SMOOTH♡
NOW DON'T BLINK...
DON'T...
BLINK
BLINK
DAMN.

SMOKEY EYES

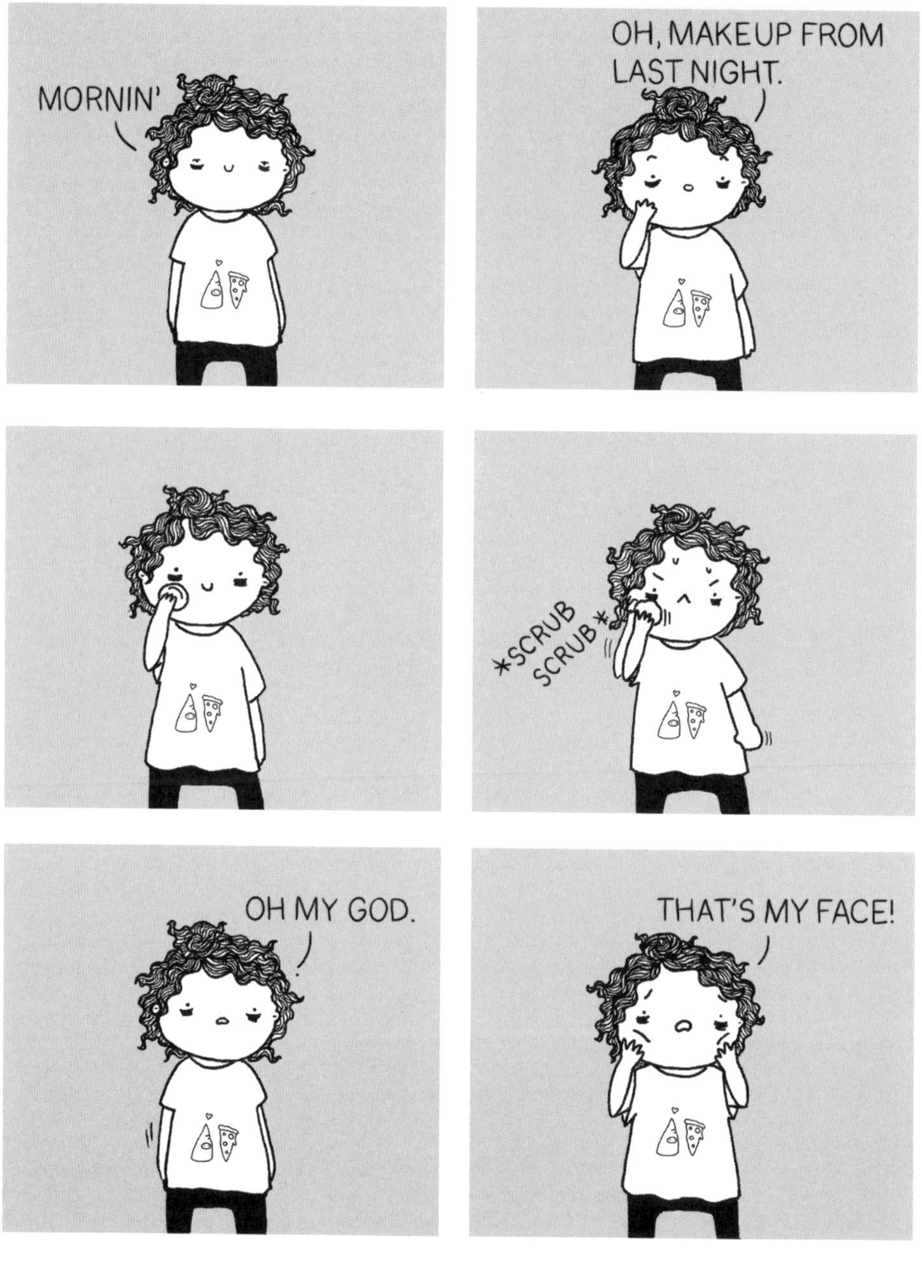
MORNIN'
OH, MAKEUP FROM LAST NIGHT.
SCRUB SCRUB
OH MY GOD.
THAT'S MY FACE!

COMFY TIME

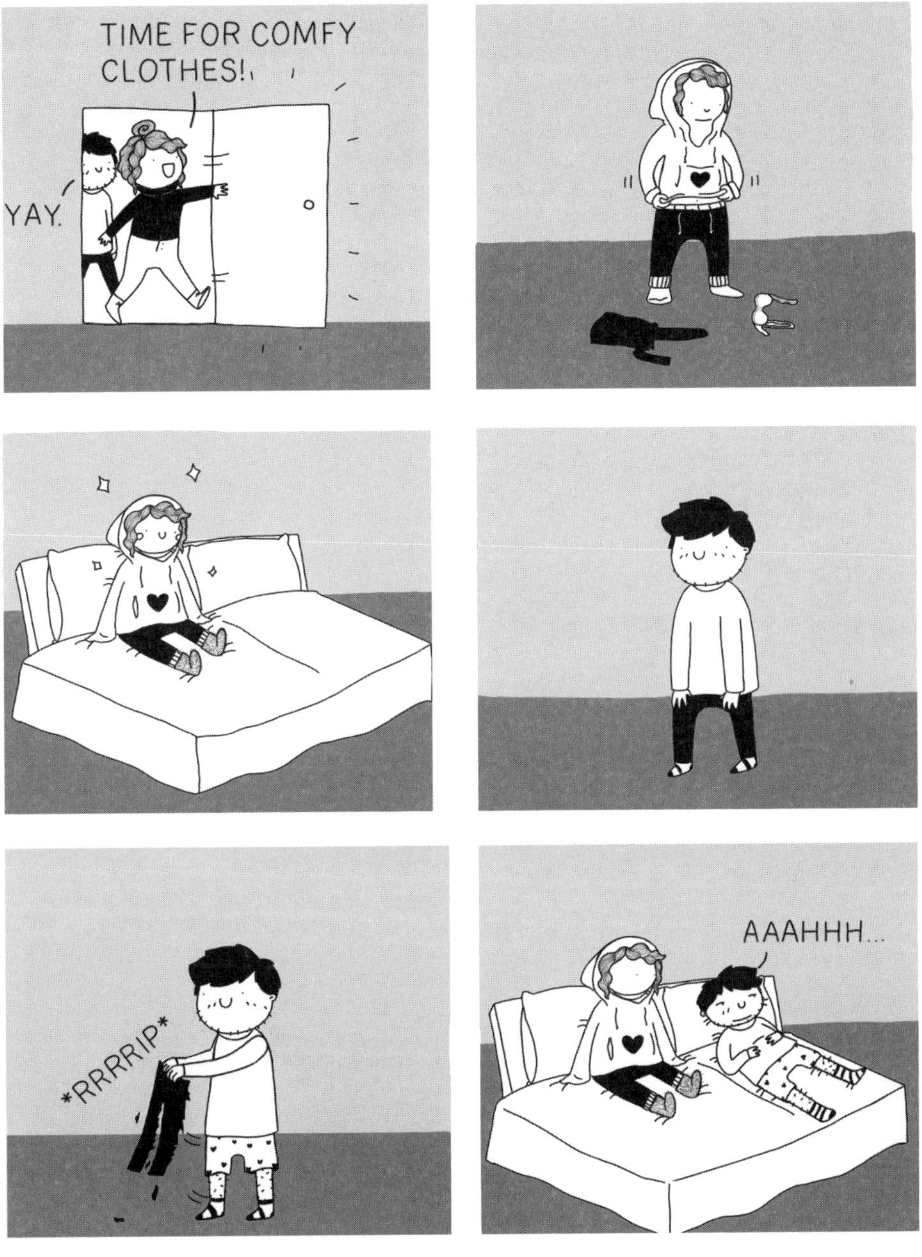
TIME FOR COMFY CLOTHES!
YAY.
RRRRIP
AAAHHH...

BLACK IS MY HAPPY COLOUR

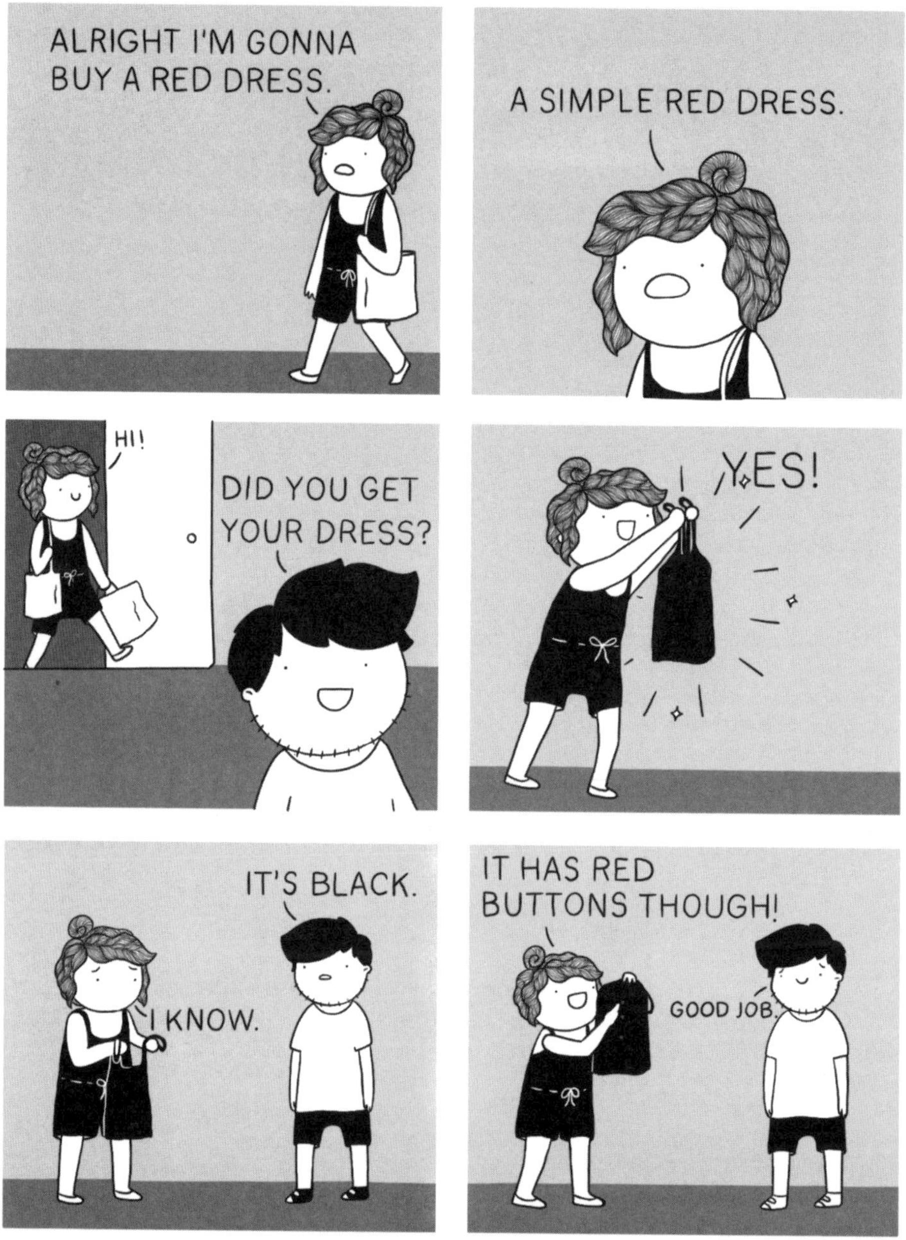
ALRIGHT I'M GONNA BUY A RED DRESS.
A SIMPLE RED DRESS.
HI!
DID YOU GET YOUR DRESS?
YES!
IT'S BLACK.
I KNOW.
IT HAS RED BUTTONS THOUGH!
GOOD JOB.

FALL

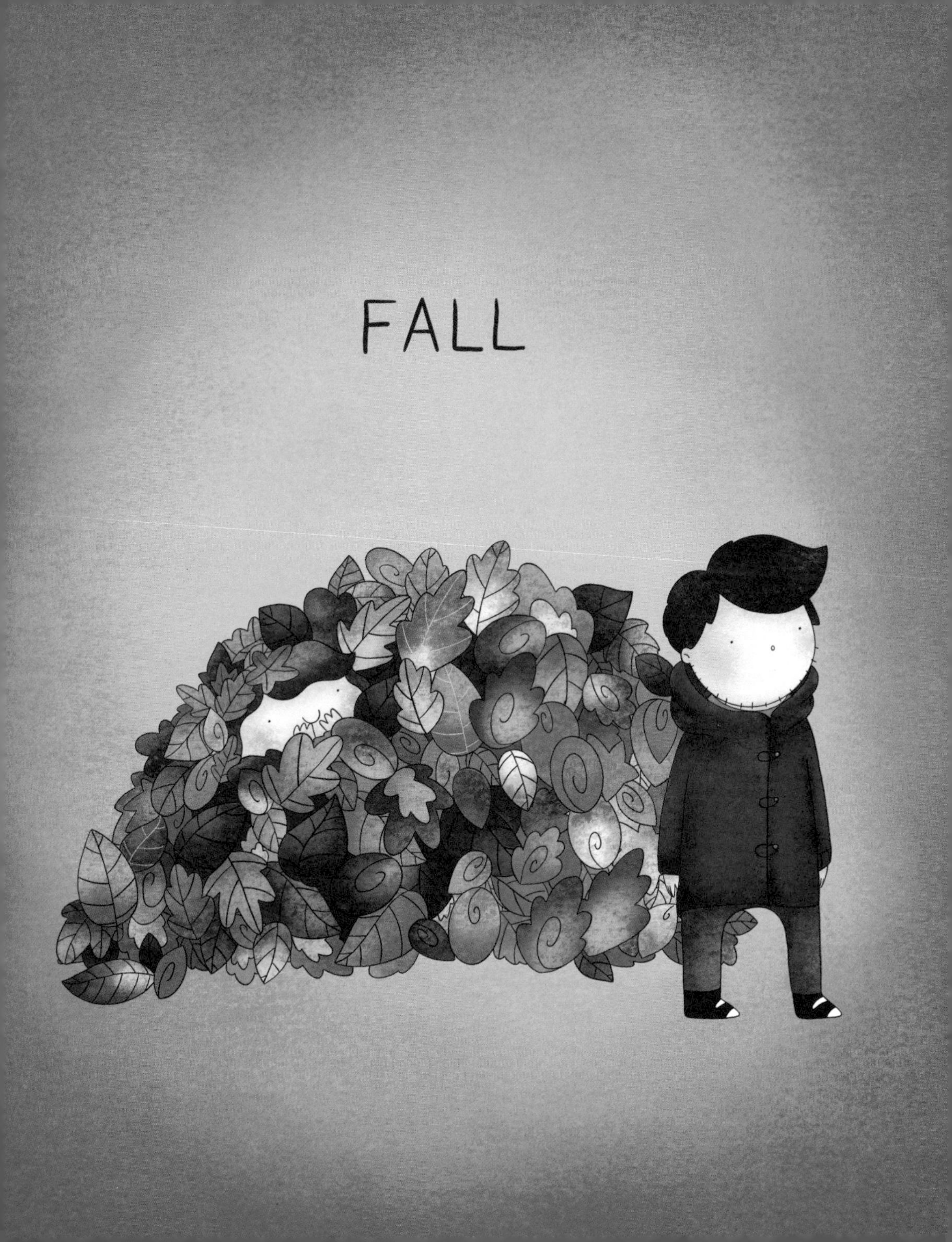

SMOL TREASURES

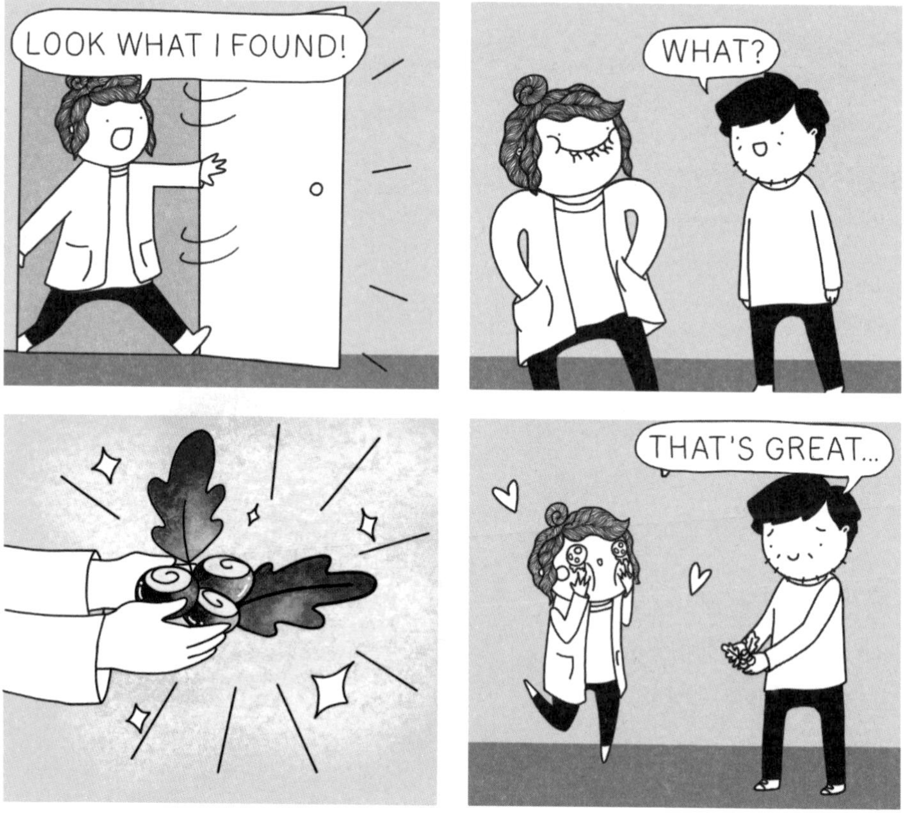
LOOK WHAT I FOUND!
WHAT?
THAT'S GREAT...

ALWAYS

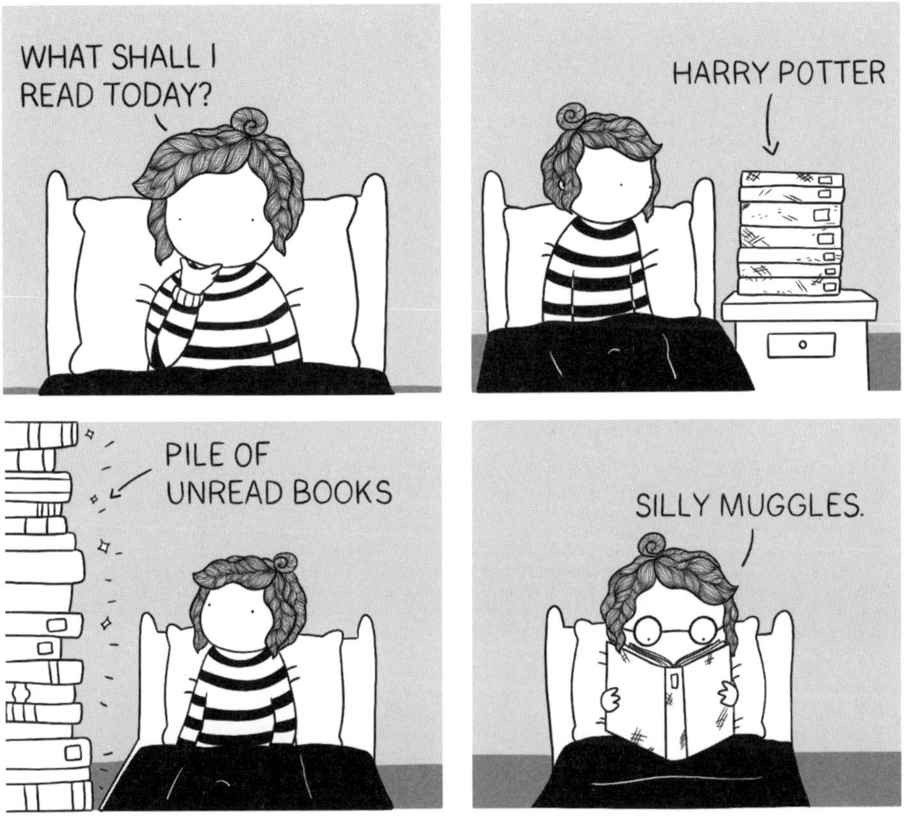
WHAT SHALL I READ TODAY?
HARRY POTTER
PILE OF UNREAD BOOKS
SILLY MUGGLES.

WHY WAIT FOR THE KNIGHT IN SHINING ARMOR

WHEN YOU CAN BE THAT KNIGHT.

WORRY NOT!
I WILL PROTECT YOU!
BONUS PANEL:
IT MOVED!
RUN! RUUUNNN!

SPOOKY

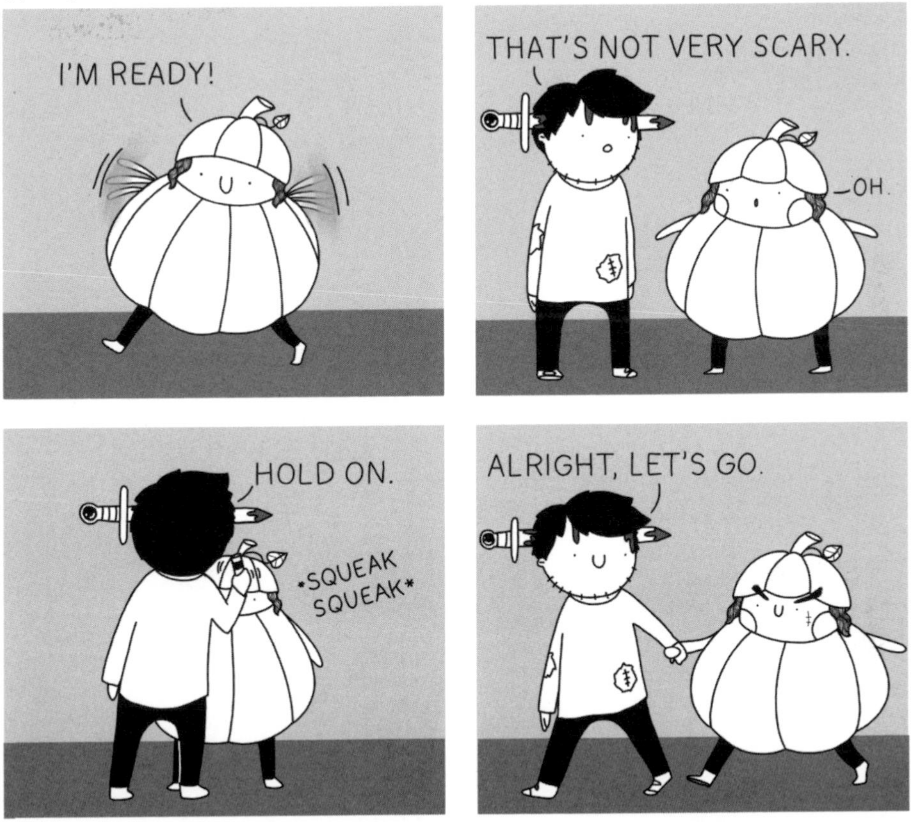
I'M READY!
THAT'S NOT VERY SCARY.
OH.
HOLD ON.
SQUEAK SQUEAK
ALRIGHT, LET'S GO.

LAST WEEK WAS CRAZY
I CAN'T WAIT TO TELL YOU ABOUT IT.
YOU'RE SUCH A GOOD LISTENER
YOU ALWAYS LISTEN.
...AND I GOT MY BACHELOR'S DEGREE.

GUIDING LIGHT

LATE NIGHT CONFESSION

GOOD NIGHT.
GOOD NIGHT.
YOU ARE MY BEST FRIEND.

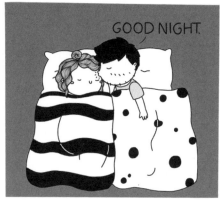

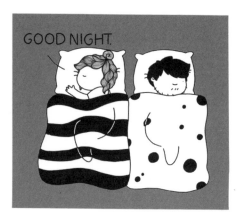

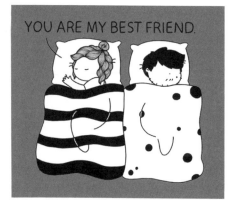

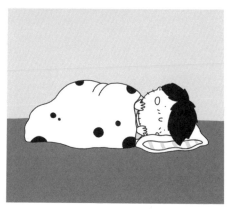

I OFTEN GET SAD

FOR NO PARTICULAR REASON

SAD COMPILATION
#57

ONE MORE LIGHT
LINKIN PARK

HOW TO SAVE A LIFE
THE FRAY

HERO OF WAR
RISE AGAINST

SNUFF
SLIPKNOT

OOOHHH. RIGHT.

DARK TIMES

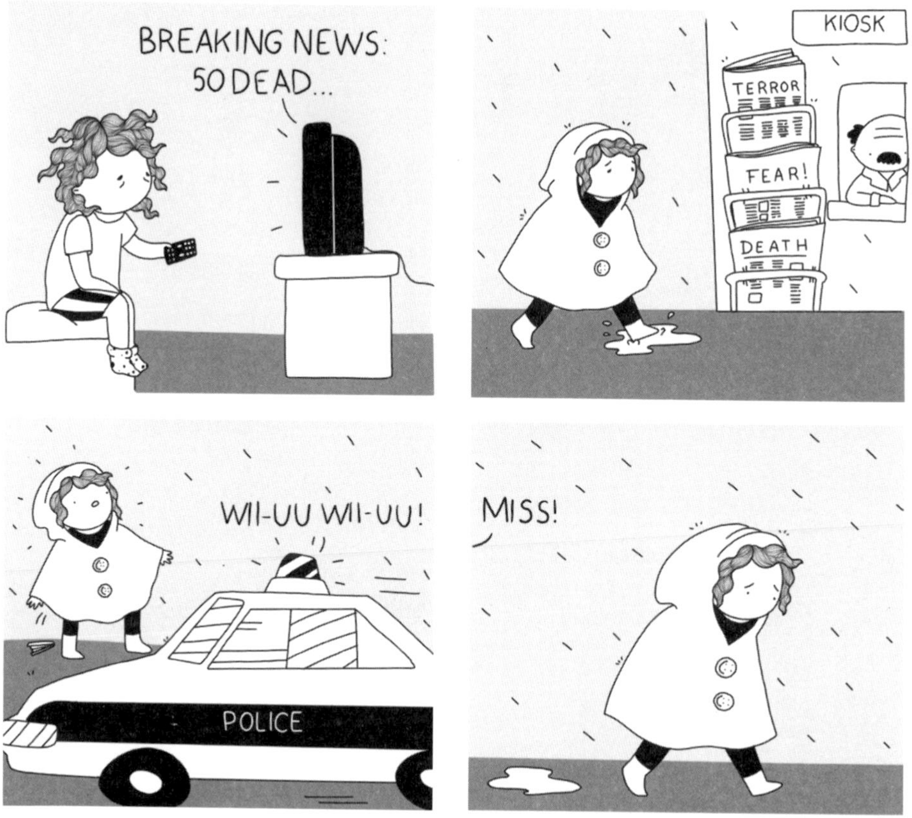
BREAKING NEWS:
50 DEAD...
KIOSK
TERROR
FEAR!
DEATH
WII-UU WII-UU!
POLICE
MISS!

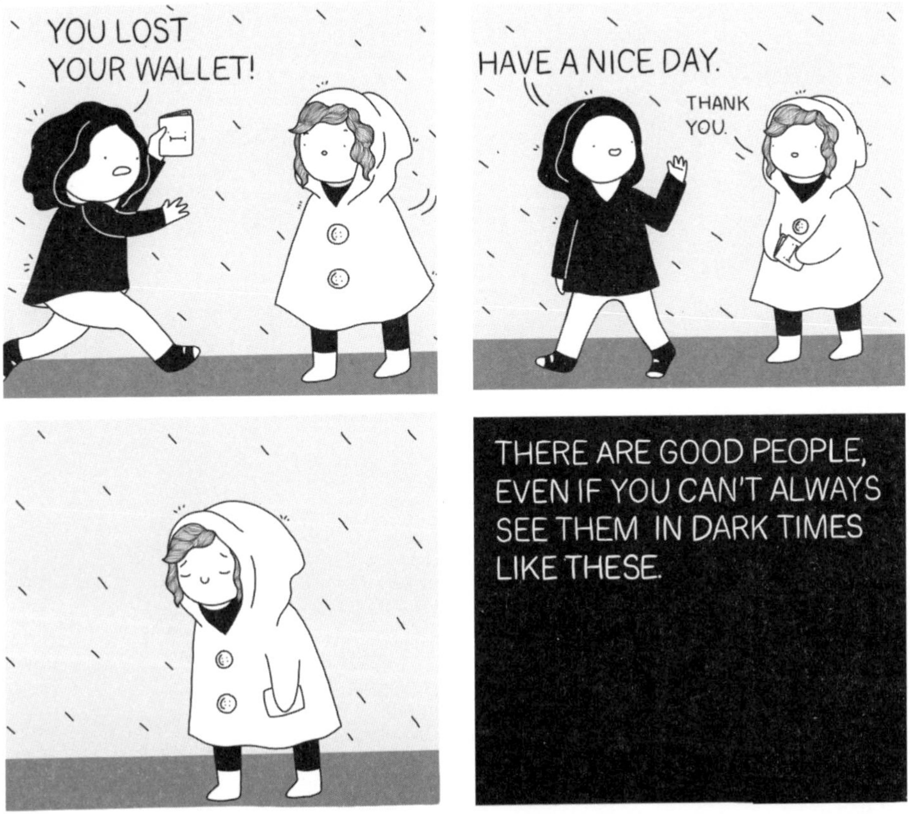
YOU LOST YOUR WALLET!
HAVE A NICE DAY.
THANK YOU.
THERE ARE GOOD PEOPLE, EVEN IF YOU CAN'T ALWAYS SEE THEM IN DARK TIMES LIKE THESE.

SMELLY LOVE

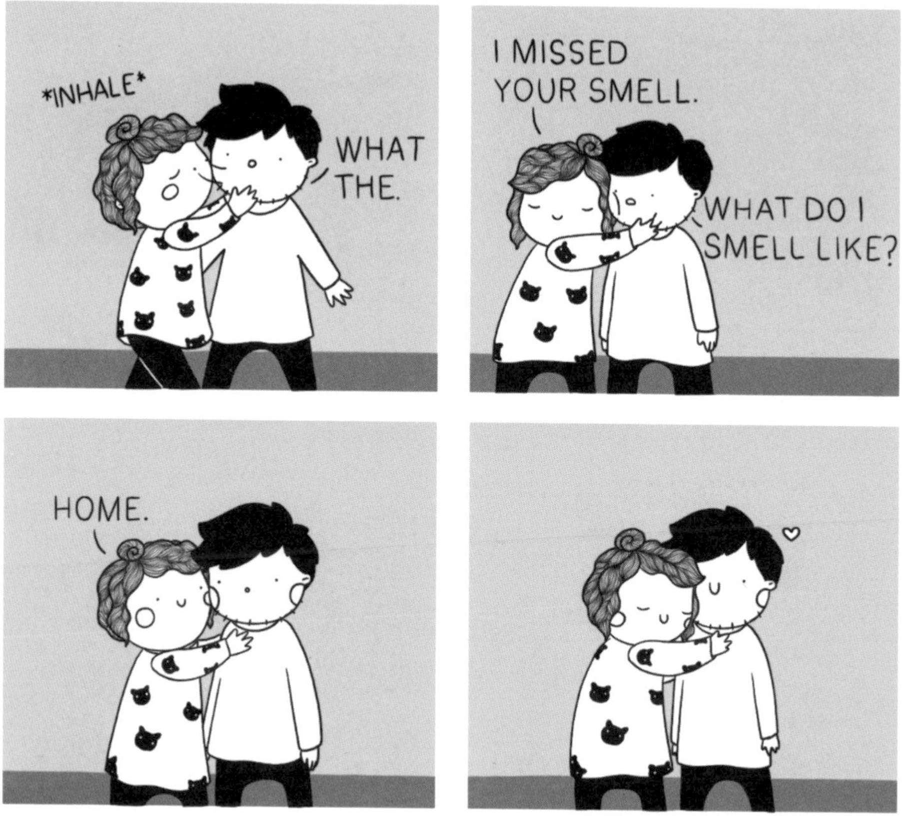
INHALE
WHAT THE.
I MISSED YOUR SMELL.
WHAT DO I SMELL LIKE?
HOME.

I CAN'T WAIT FOR TONIGHT

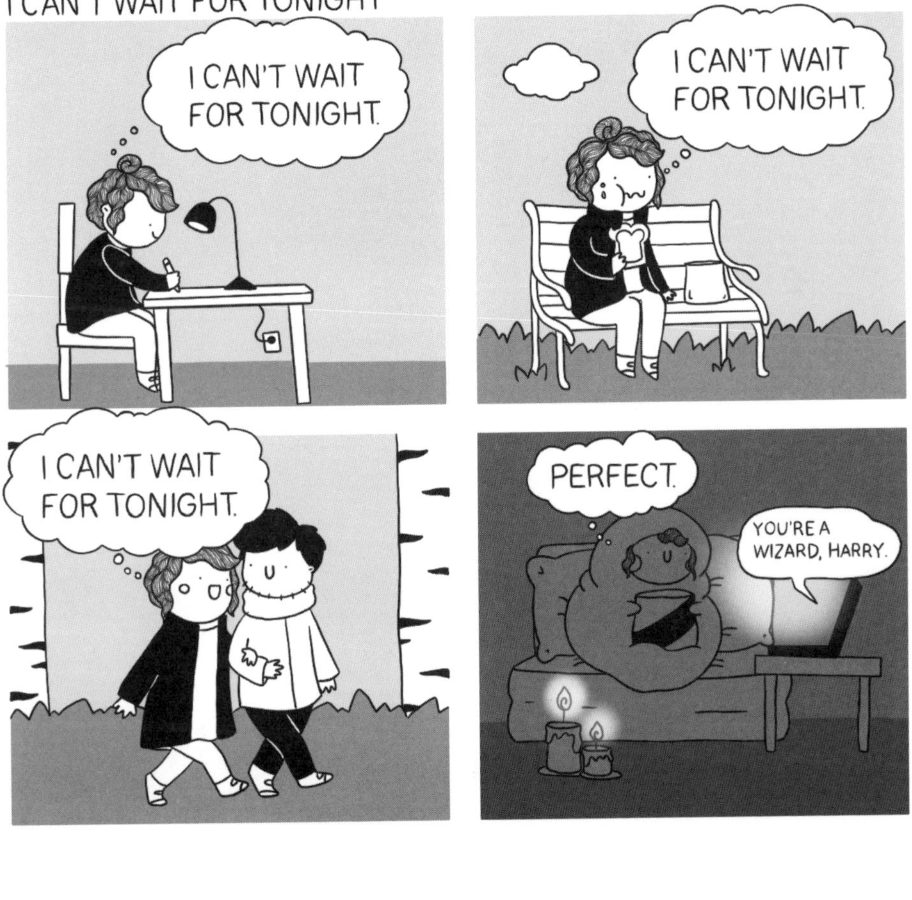
I CAN'T WAIT FOR TONIGHT.
I CAN'T WAIT FOR TONIGHT.
I CAN'T WAIT FOR TONIGHT.
PERFECT.
YOU'RE A WIZARD, HARRY.

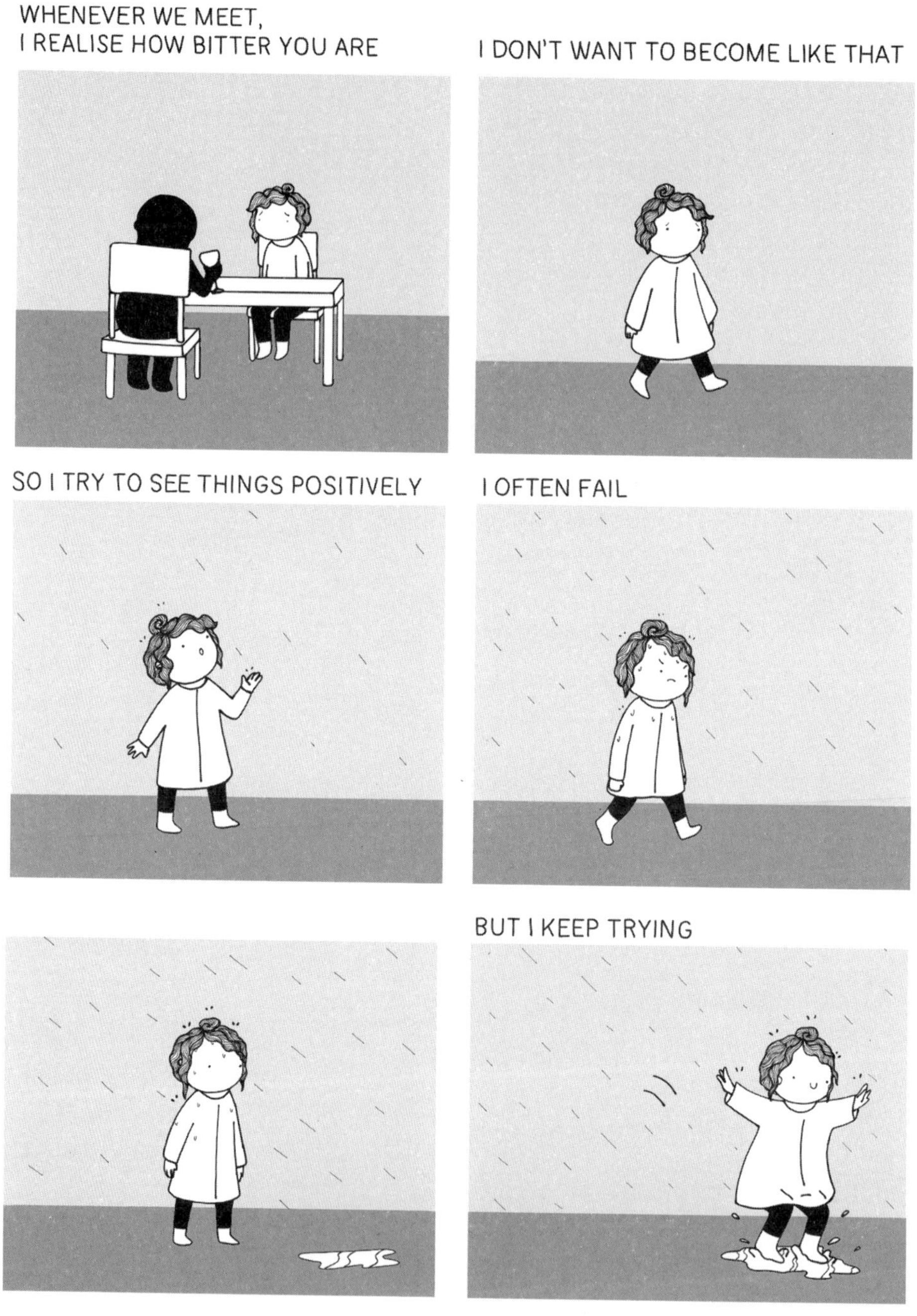
WHENEVER WE MEET,
I REALISE HOW BITTER YOU ARE
I DON'T WANT TO BECOME LIKE THAT
SO I TRY TO SEE THINGS POSITIVELY
I OFTEN FAIL
BUT I KEEP TRYING

MOOOAAAR

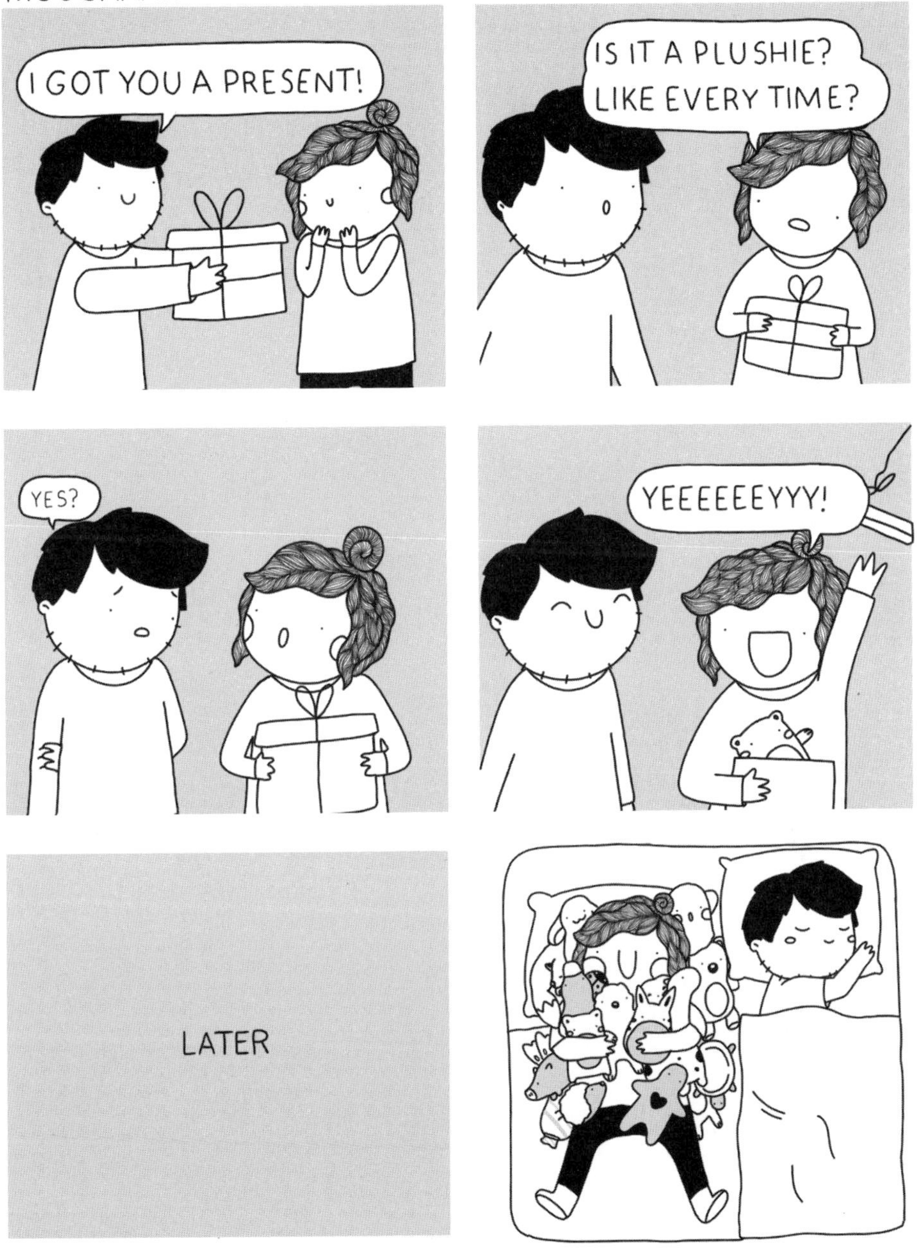
I GOT YOU A PRESENT!
IS IT A PLUSHIE? LIKE EVERY TIME?
YES?
YEEEEEEYYY!
LATER

TEA TIME

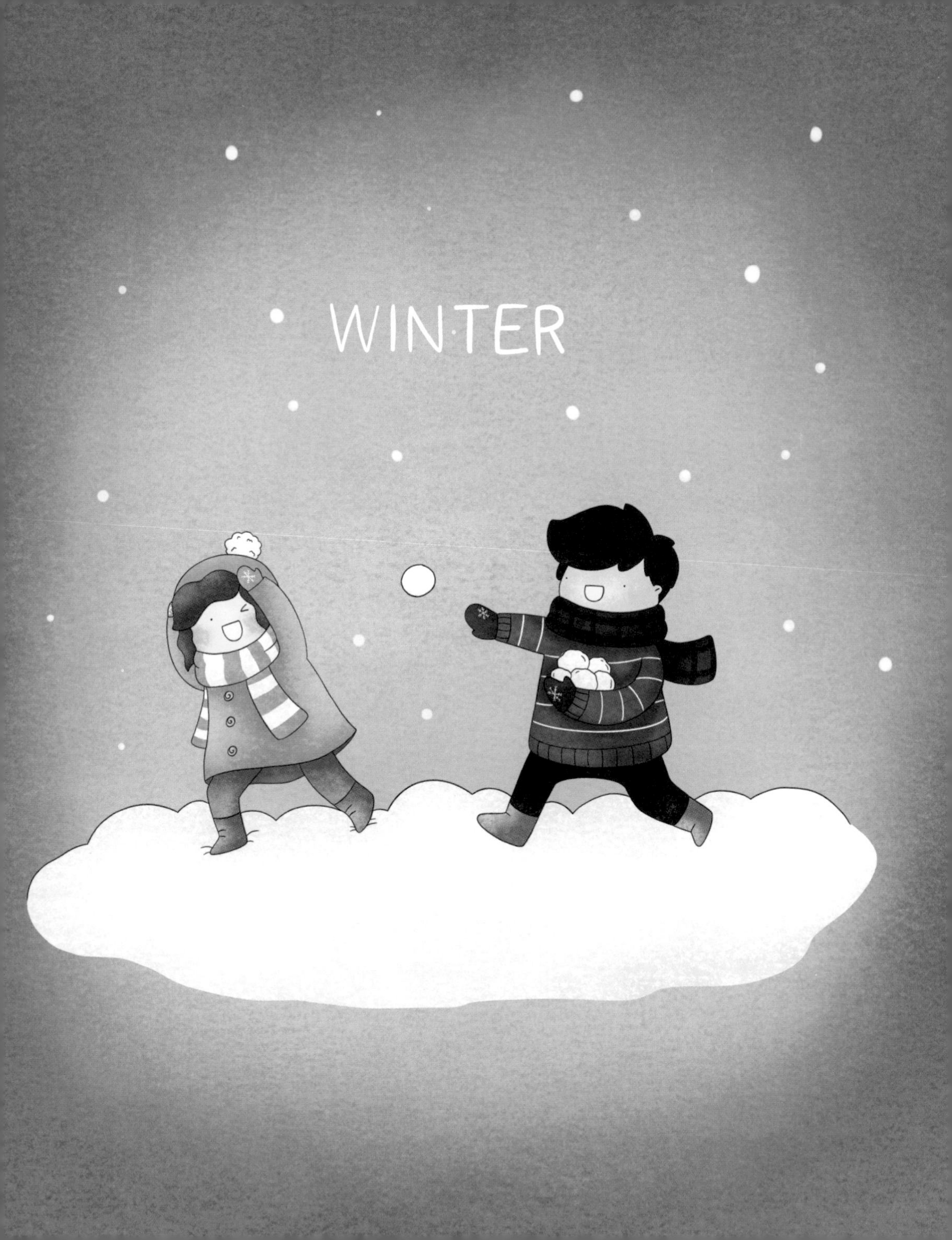
WINTER

TRUE JOY

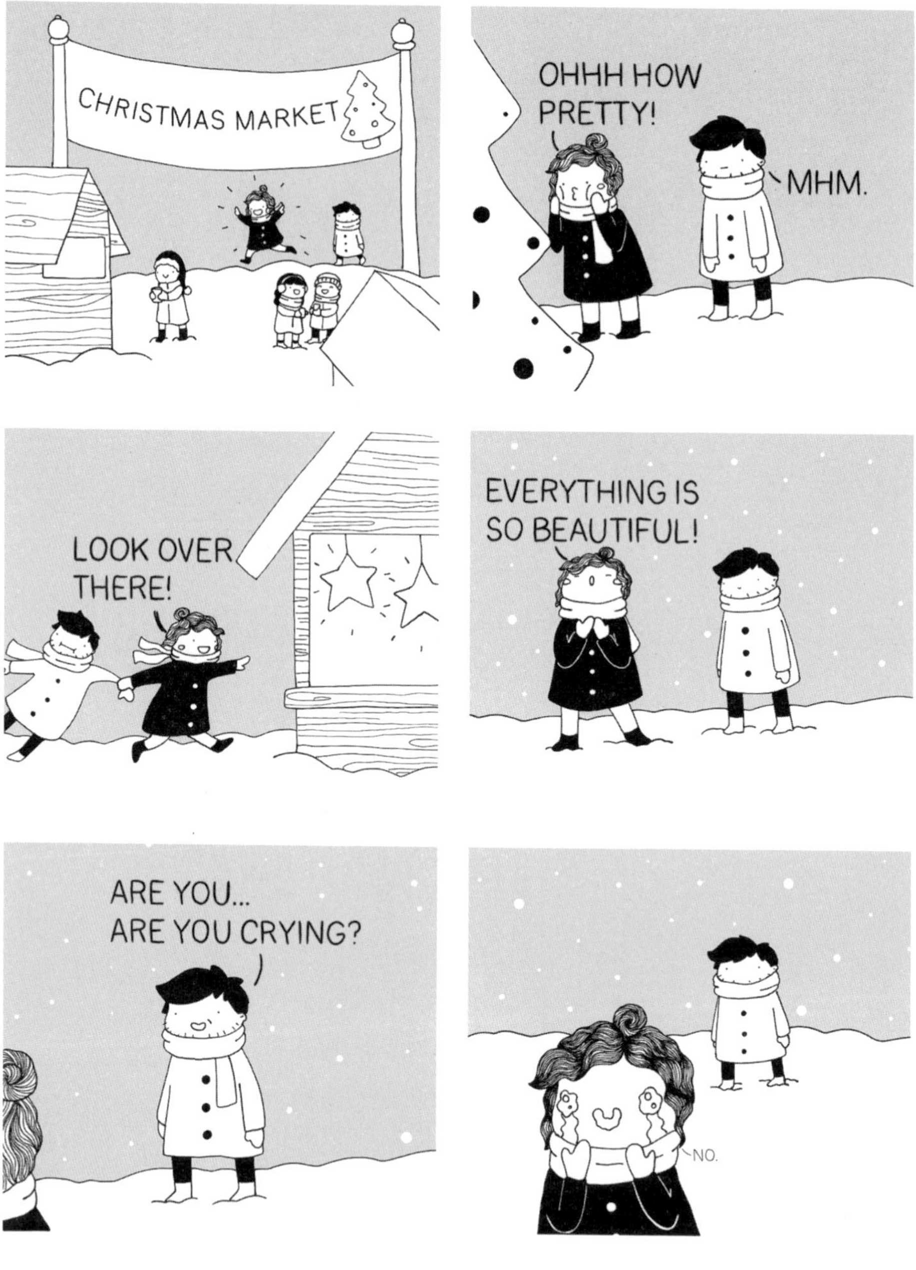
CHRISTMAS MARKET
OHHH HOW PRETTY!
MHM.
LOOK OVER THERE!
EVERYTHING IS SO BEAUTIFUL!
ARE YOU...
ARE YOU CRYING?
NO.

CLUMSY

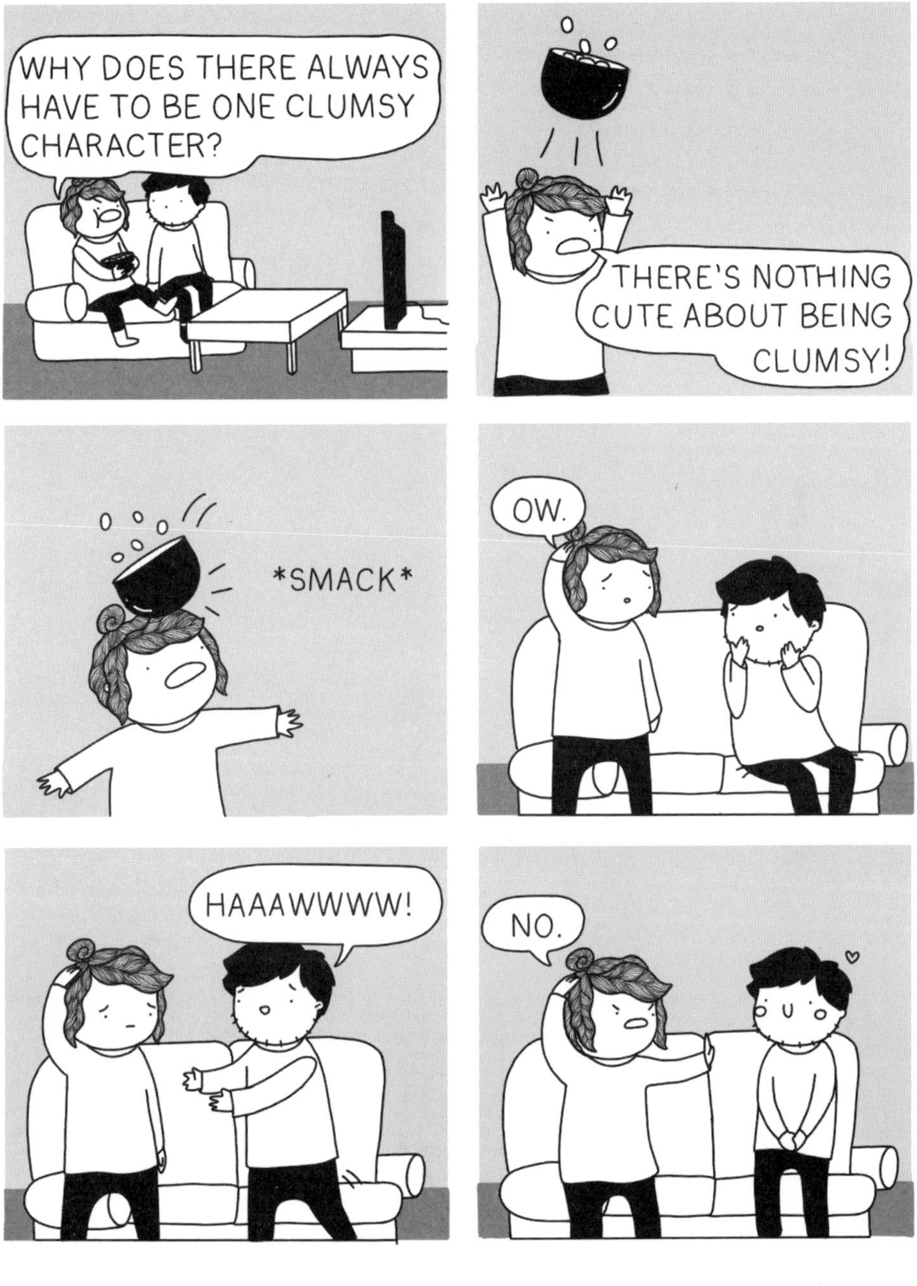
WHY DOES THERE ALWAYS HAVE TO BE ONE CLUMSY CHARACTER?
THERE'S NOTHING CUTE ABOUT BEING CLUMSY!
SMACK
OW.
HAAAWWWW!
NO.

GUIDE

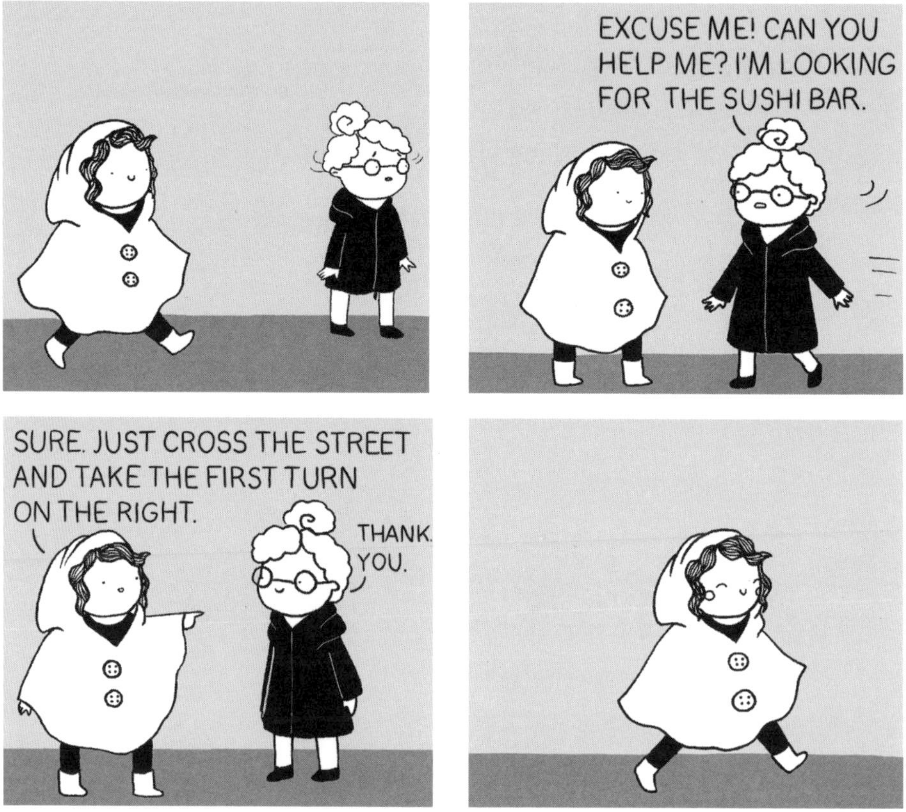
EXCUSE ME! CAN YOU HELP ME? I'M LOOKING FOR THE SUSHI BAR.
SURE. JUST CROSS THE STREET AND TAKE THE FIRST TURN ON THE RIGHT.
THANK. YOU.

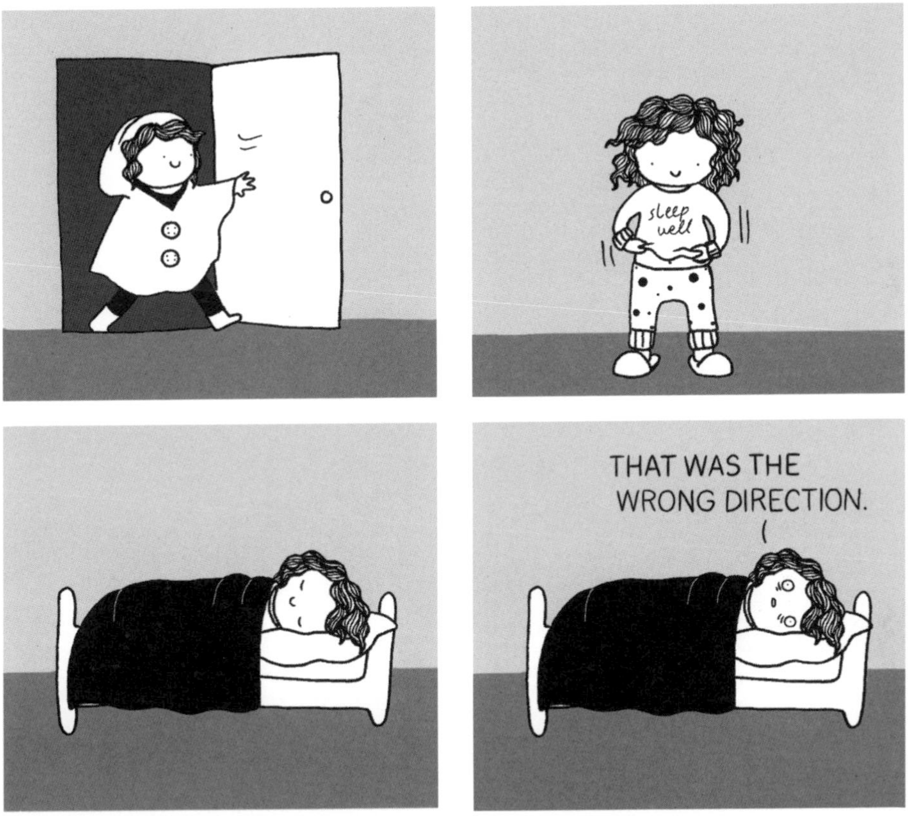
sleep well
THAT WAS THE WRONG DIRECTION.

MOOD SWINGS

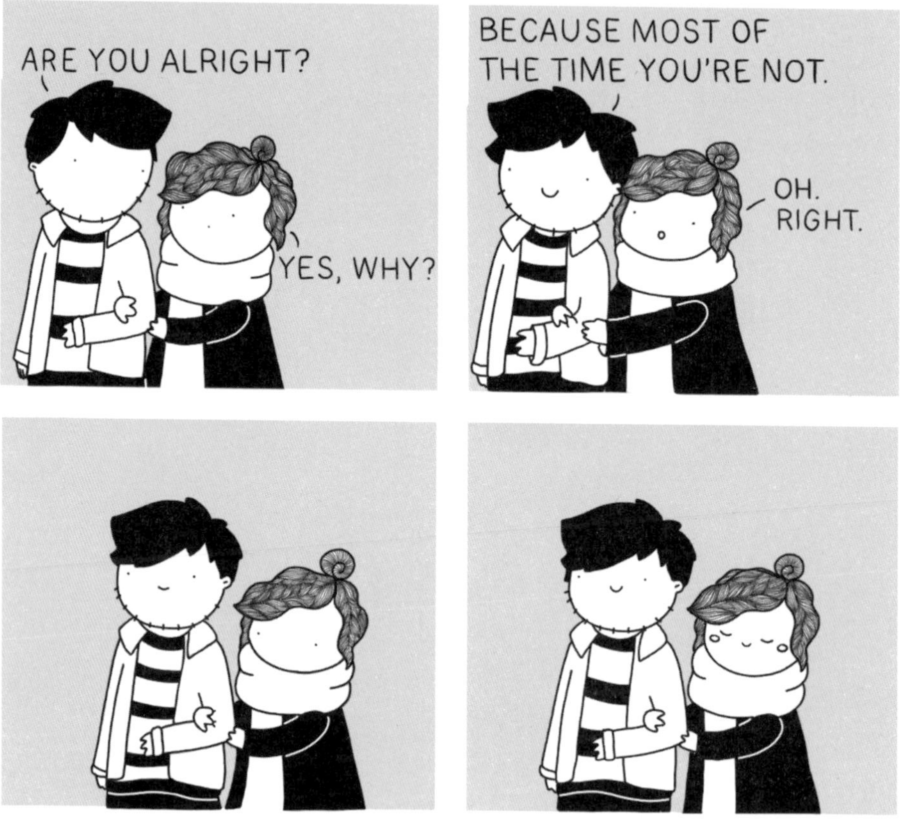
ARE YOU ALRIGHT?
YES, WHY?
BECAUSE MOST OF THE TIME YOU'RE NOT.
OH. RIGHT.

ATTENTION CRAVER

GIVE ME ATTENTION.

DON'T

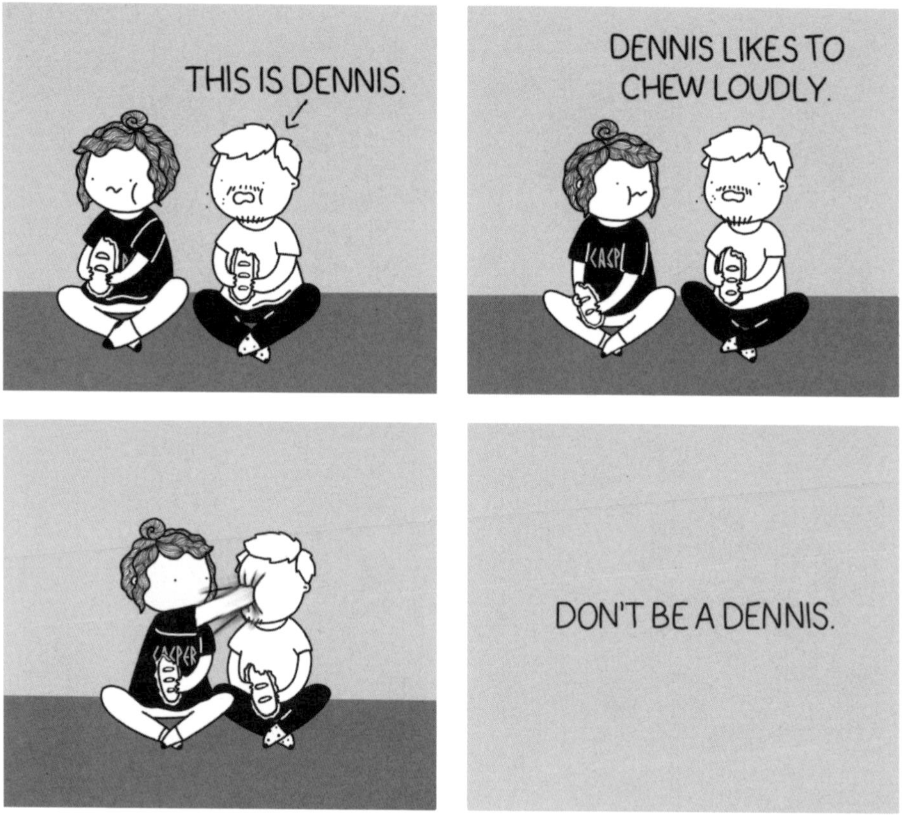

THIS IS DENNIS.
DENNIS LIKES TO CHEW LOUDLY.
DON'T BE A DENNIS.

SUCKER FOR CHRISTMAS

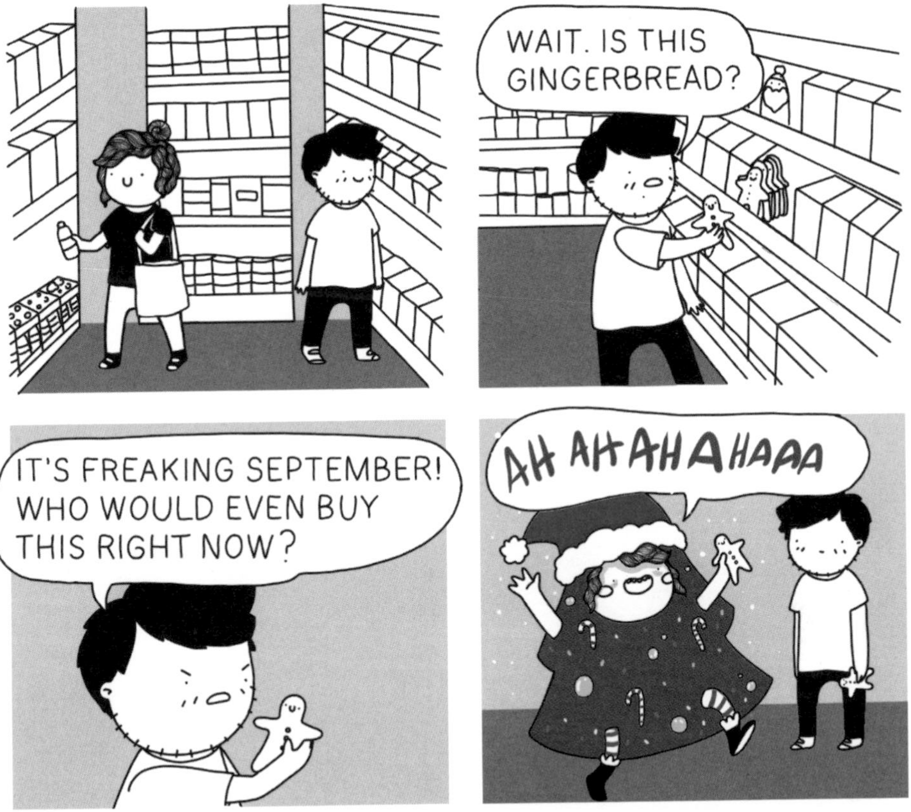
WAIT. IS THIS GINGERBREAD?
IT'S FREAKING SEPTEMBER! WHO WOULD EVEN BUY THIS RIGHT NOW?
AH AHAHAHAHAAA

SELFLESS

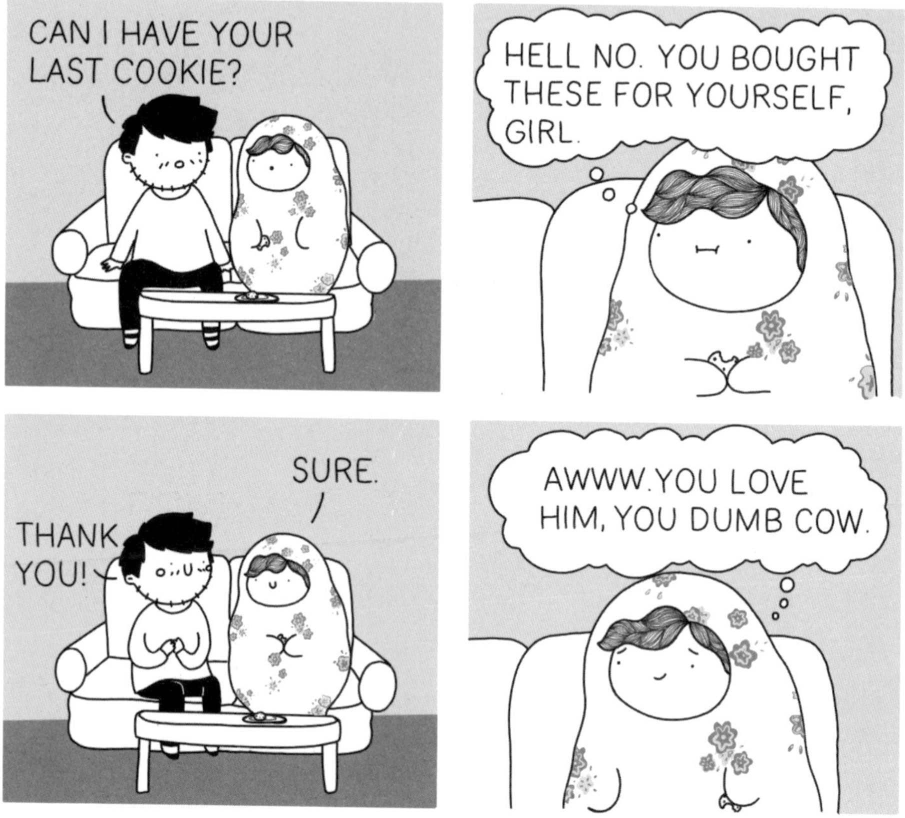
CAN I HAVE YOUR LAST COOKIE?
HELL NO. YOU BOUGHT THESE FOR YOURSELF, GIRL.
SURE.
THANK YOU!
AWWW. YOU LOVE HIM, YOU DUMB COW.

SHY GUY

BLABLA
CHATTER
HAHA!
RIGHT?
YOUR BOYFRIEND IS MORE THE QUIET TYPE, HUH?
YEAH...
AT HOME
WUUUIIII! LULULU!

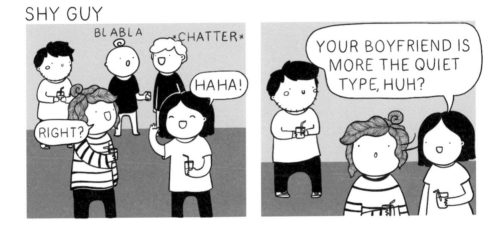

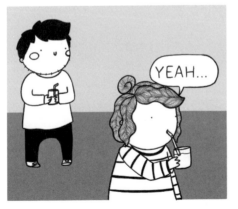

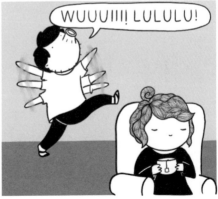

PERFECT GIFT

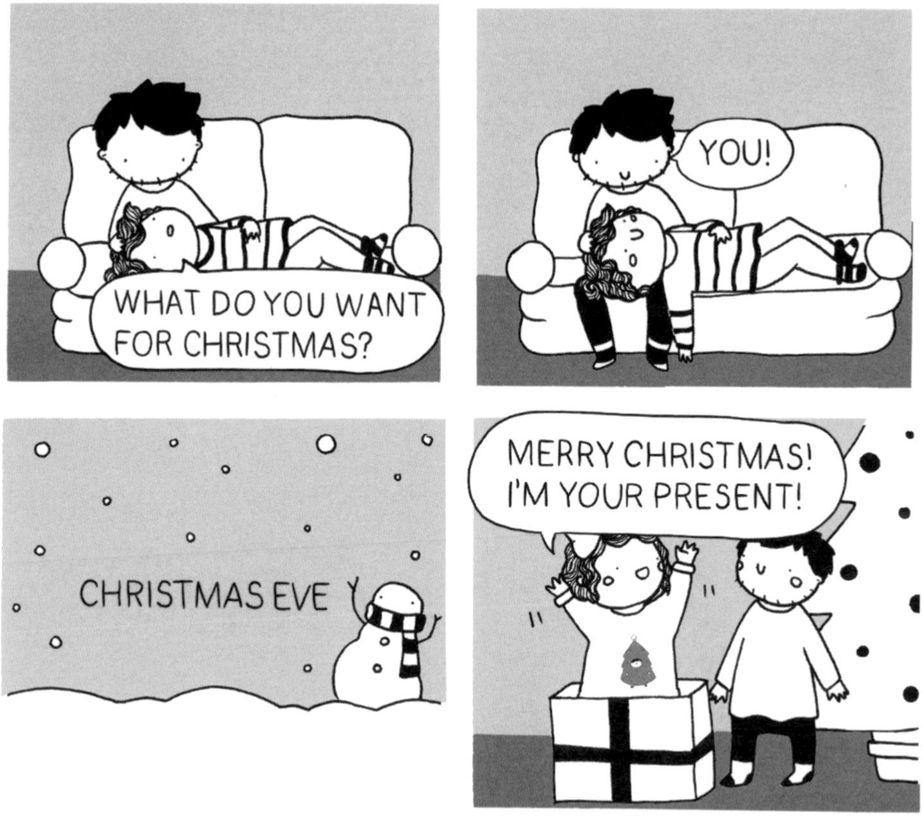
WHAT DO YOU WANT FOR CHRISTMAS?
YOU!
CHRISTMAS EVE
MERRY CHRISTMAS! I'M YOUR PRESENT!

EXACTLY WHAT I WANTED!
TIHI.
THE END
WAIT. SO YOU DIDN'T GET ME ANY REAL PRESENTS?
THE END.

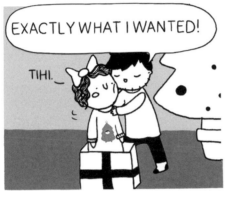

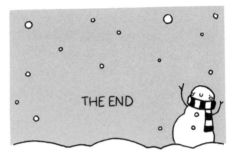

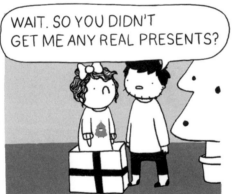

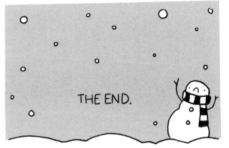

TOY STORY

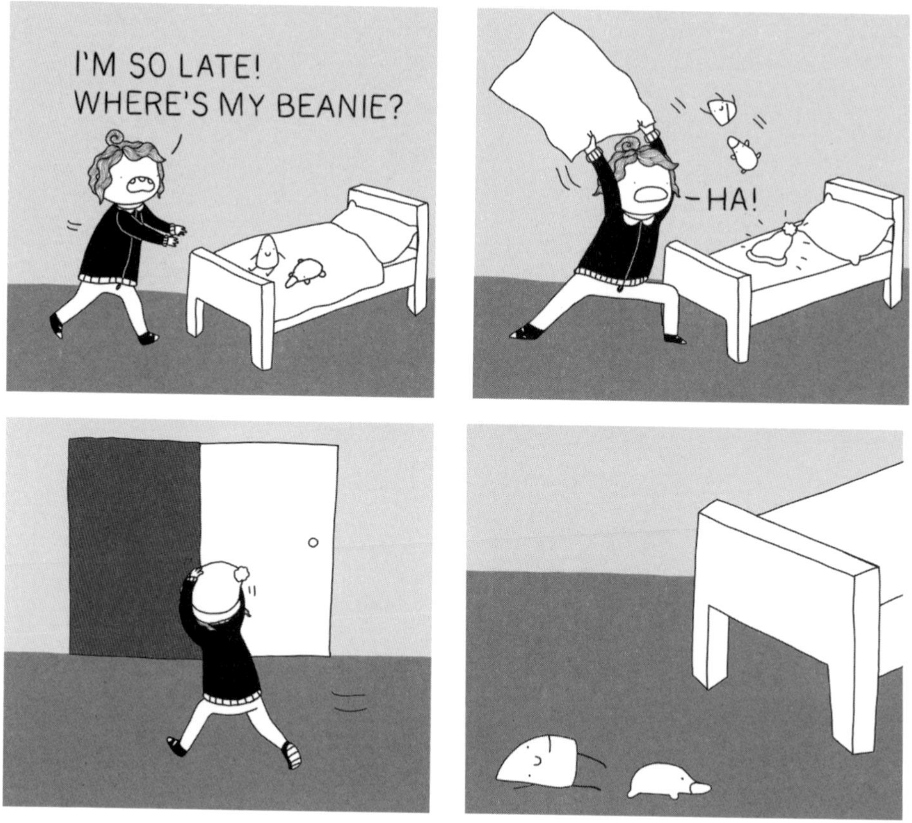
I'M SO LATE!
WHERE'S MY BEANIE?
HA!

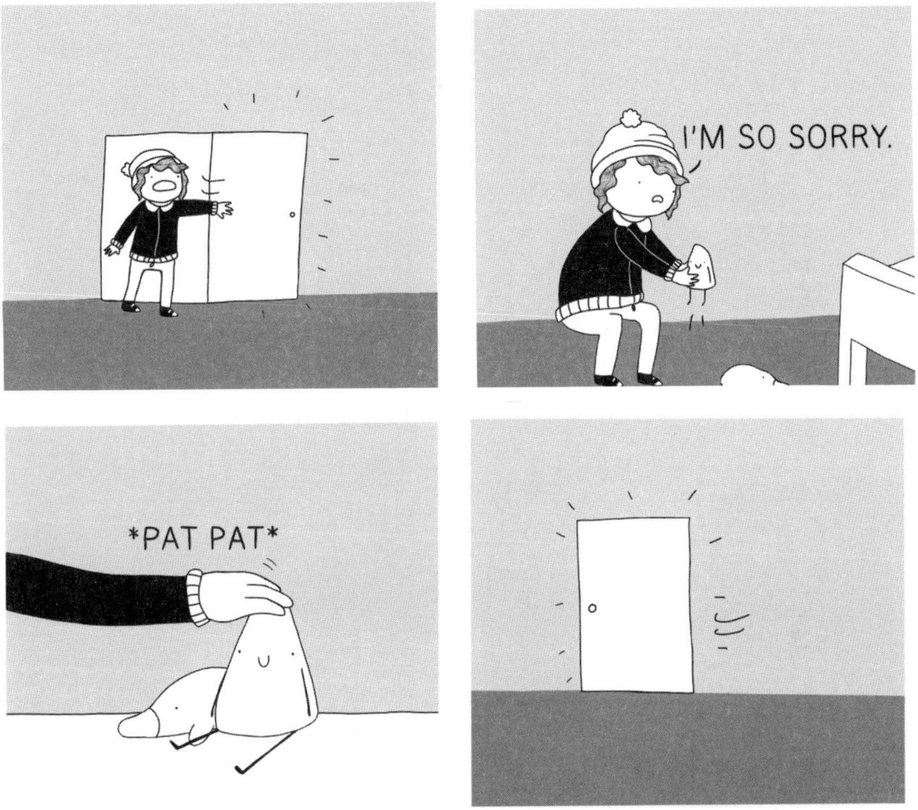
I'M SO SORRY.
PAT PAT

WAKING UP NEXT TO HIM

ALWAYS COLD

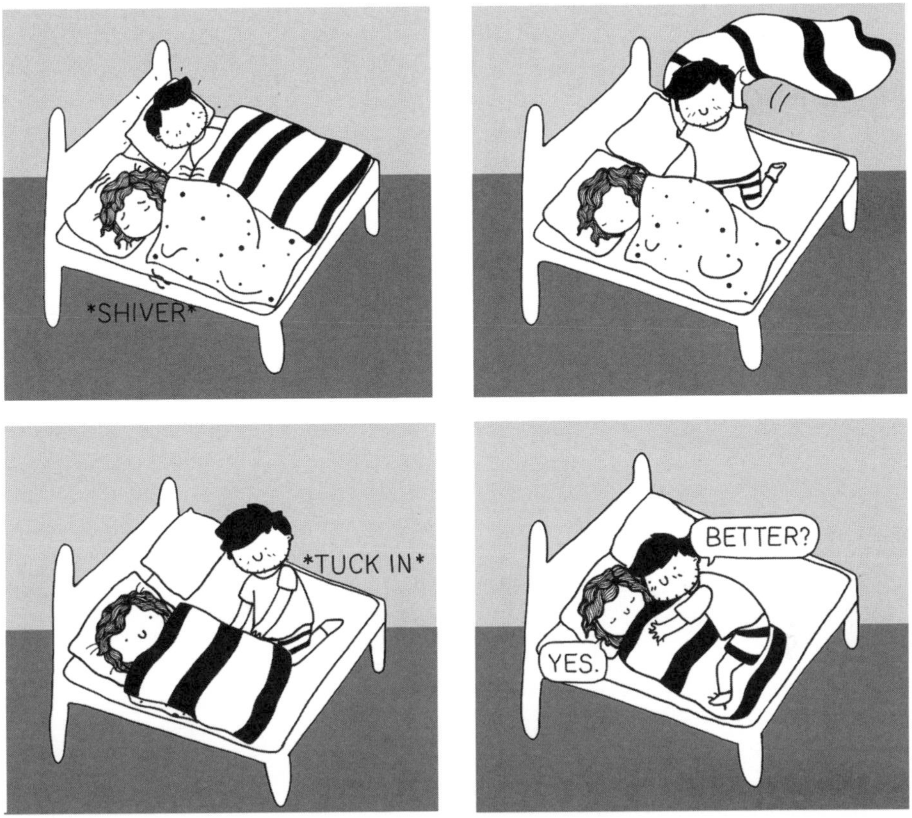
SHIVER
TUCK IN
BETTER?
YES.

NEW YEAR'S EVE

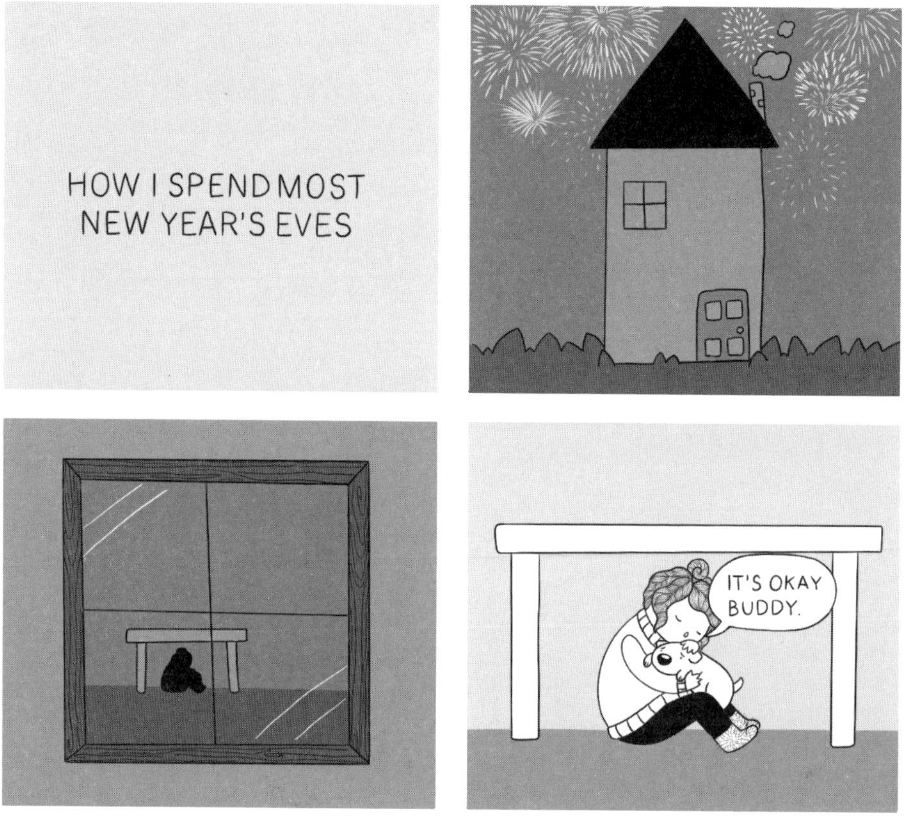
HOW I SPEND MOST NEW YEAR'S EVES
IT'S OKAY BUDDY.

NEW COMICS

BAD POSTURE

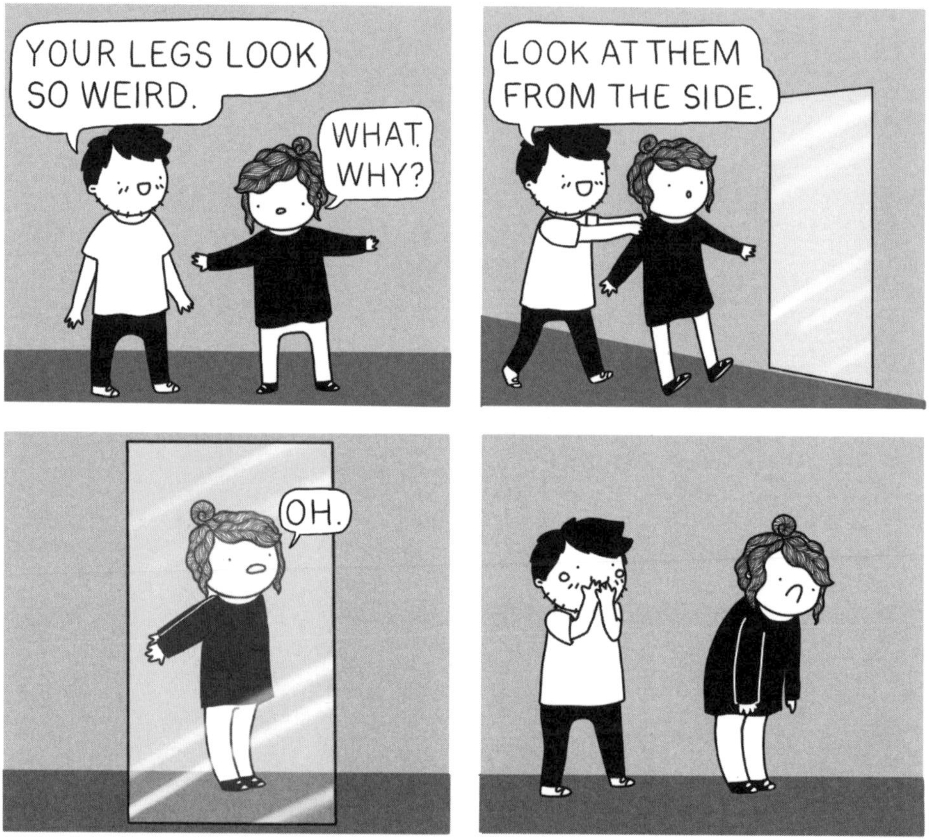
YOUR LEGS LOOK SO WEIRD.
WHAT. WHY?
LOOK AT THEM FROM THE SIDE.
OH.

COMFORT ZONE

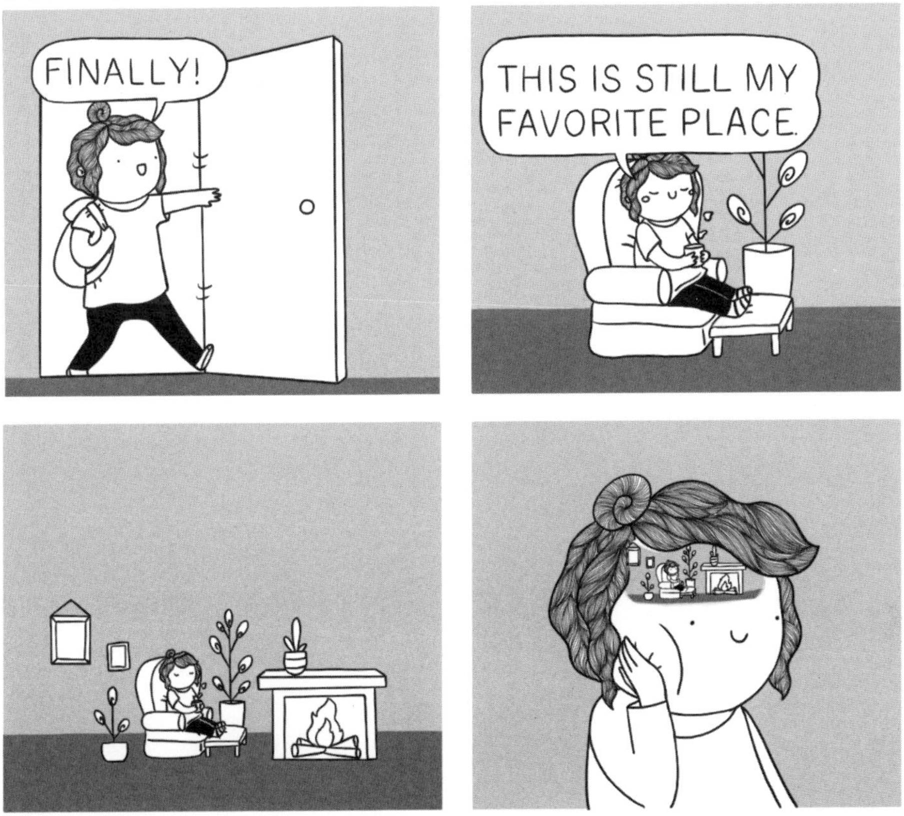
FINALLY!
THIS IS STILL MY FAVORITE PLACE.

GOOD OLD TIMES

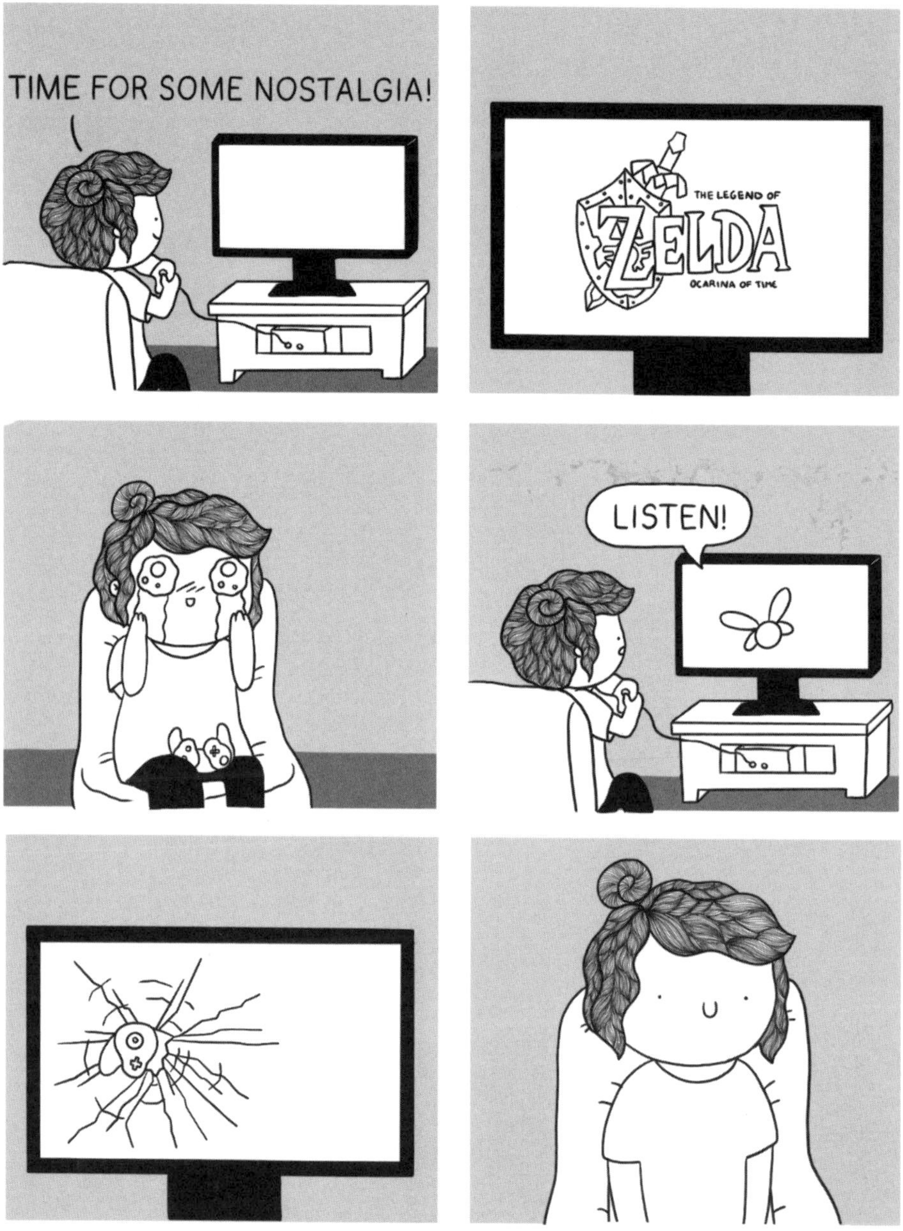
TIME FOR SOME NOSTALGIA!
THE LEGEND OF
ZELDA
OCARINA OF TIME
LISTEN!

MOST WONDERFUL SOUND

IT'S SNOWING!
OK THIS IS IT.
THE MOMENT.
CRRRUNSH
YESSS.

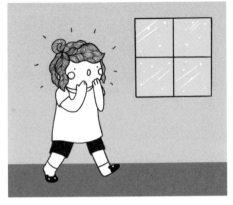

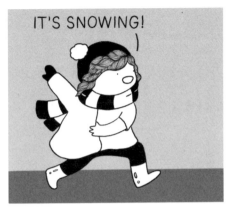

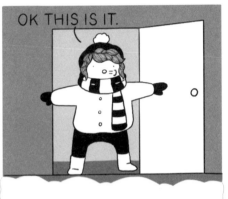

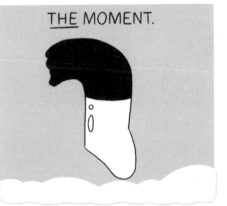

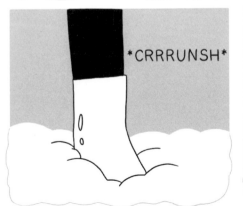

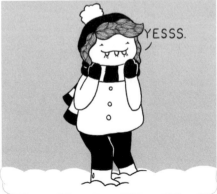

MAKE YOU FEEL BETTER

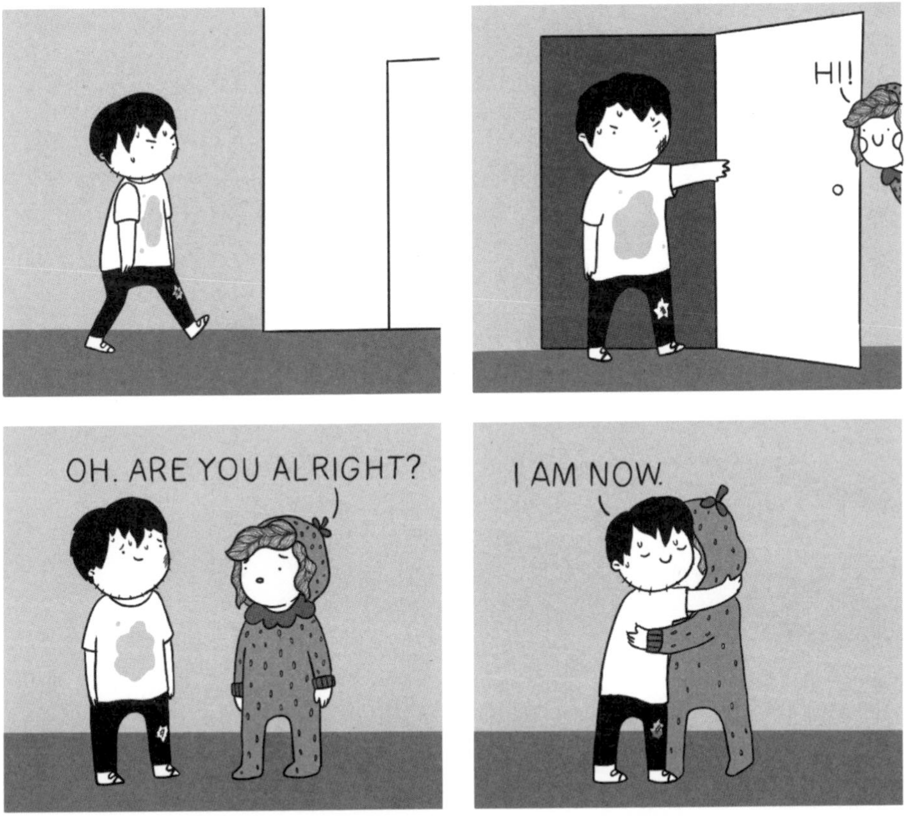
HI!
OH. ARE YOU ALRIGHT?
I AM NOW.

BALANCE

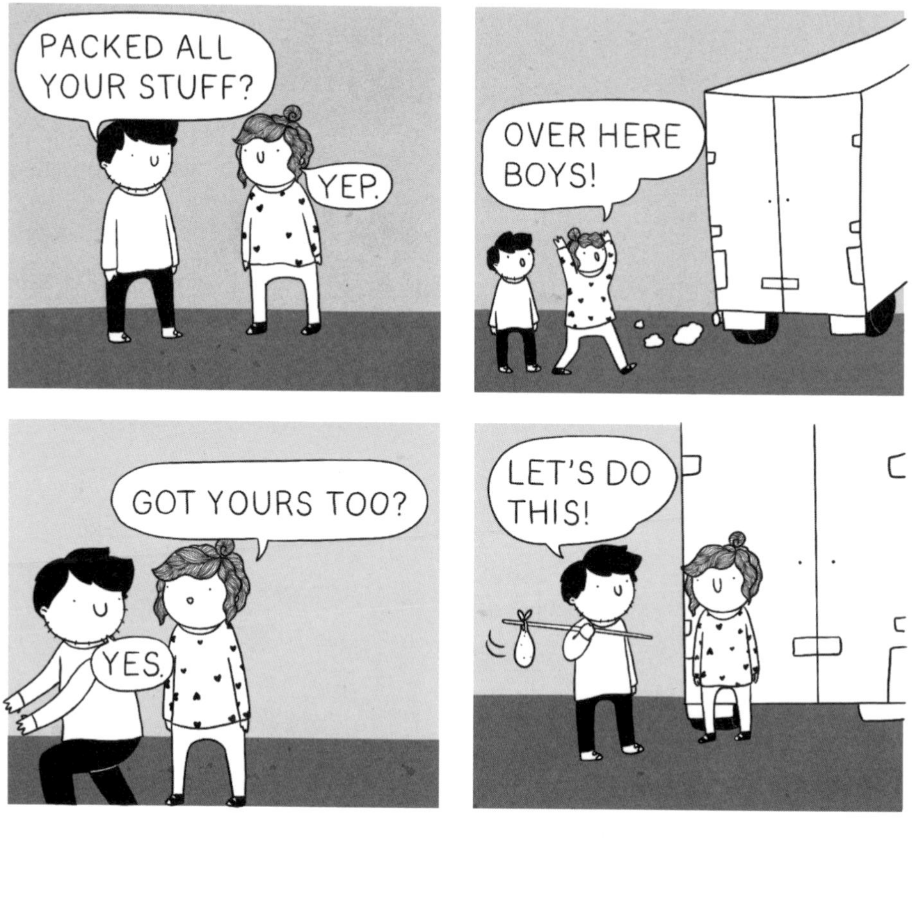
PACKED ALL YOUR STUFF?
YEP.
OVER HERE BOYS!
GOT YOURS TOO?
YES.
LET'S DO THIS!

BEST FRIEND

CARETAKER

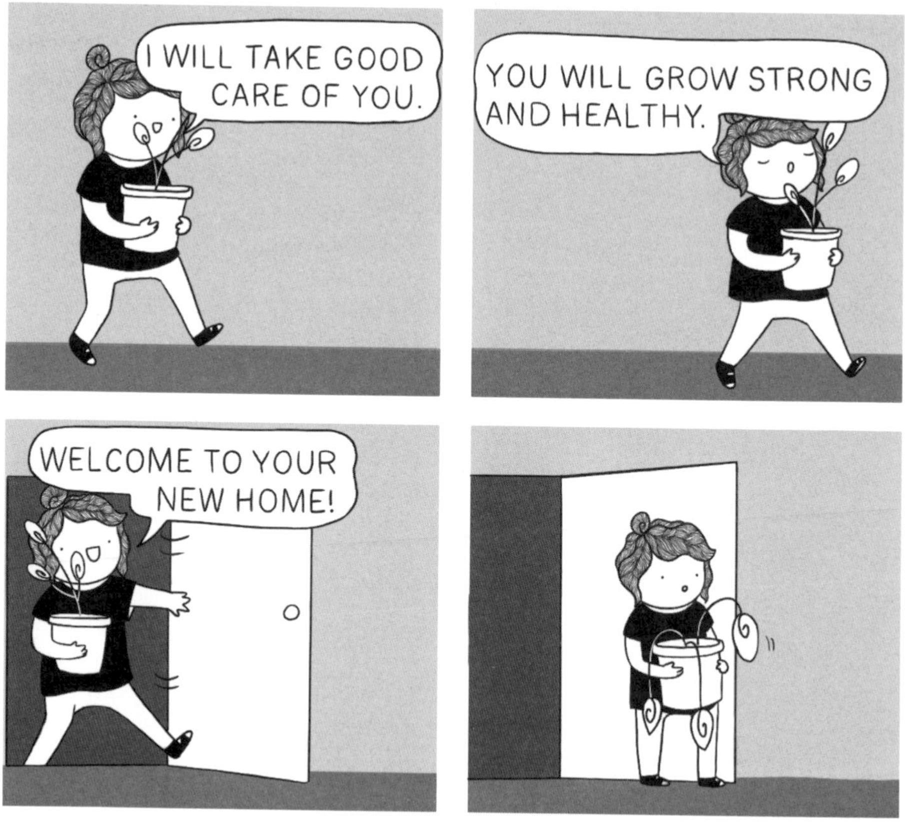
I WILL TAKE GOOD CARE OF YOU.
YOU WILL GROW STRONG AND HEALTHY.
WELCOME TO YOUR NEW HOME!

FIRST SNOW

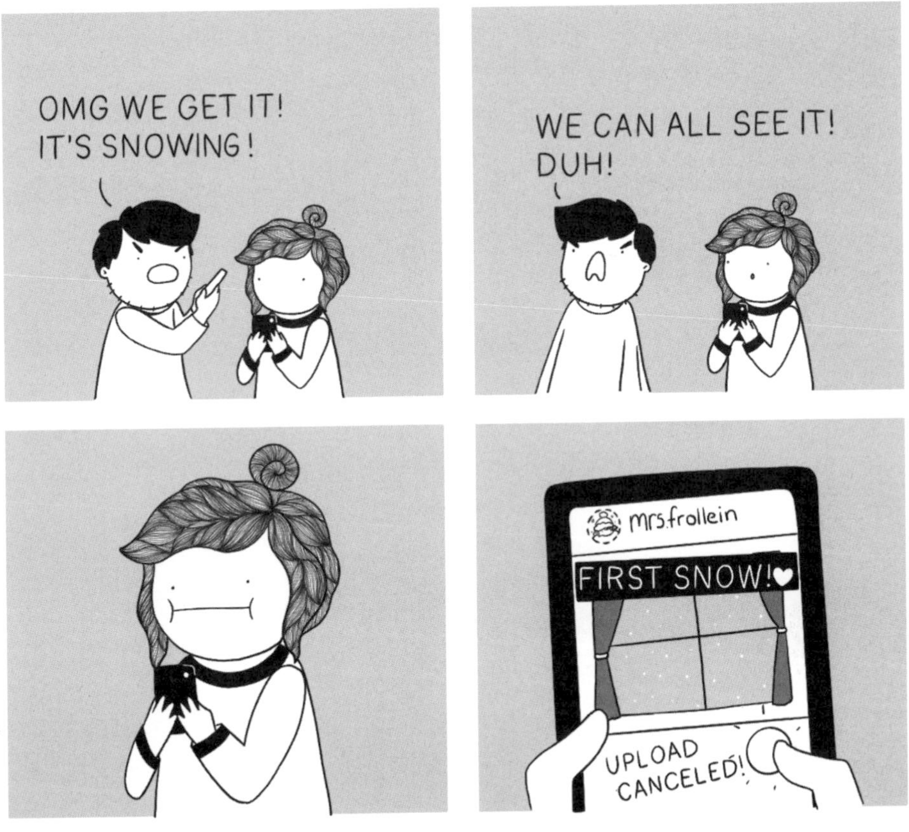
OMG WE GET IT! IT'S SNOWING!
WE CAN ALL SEE IT! DUH!
mrs.frollein
FIRST SNOW!
UPLOAD CANCELED!

FORM FOLLOWS FUNCTION

ISN'T IT CRAZY HOW PEOPLE ARE DESIGNED...
...TO FIT PERFECTLY INTO EACH OTHER.
YOU KNOW WHAT I MEAN, RIGHT?
Y...YES?
LOOK! PERFECT FIT!

FULL MOON

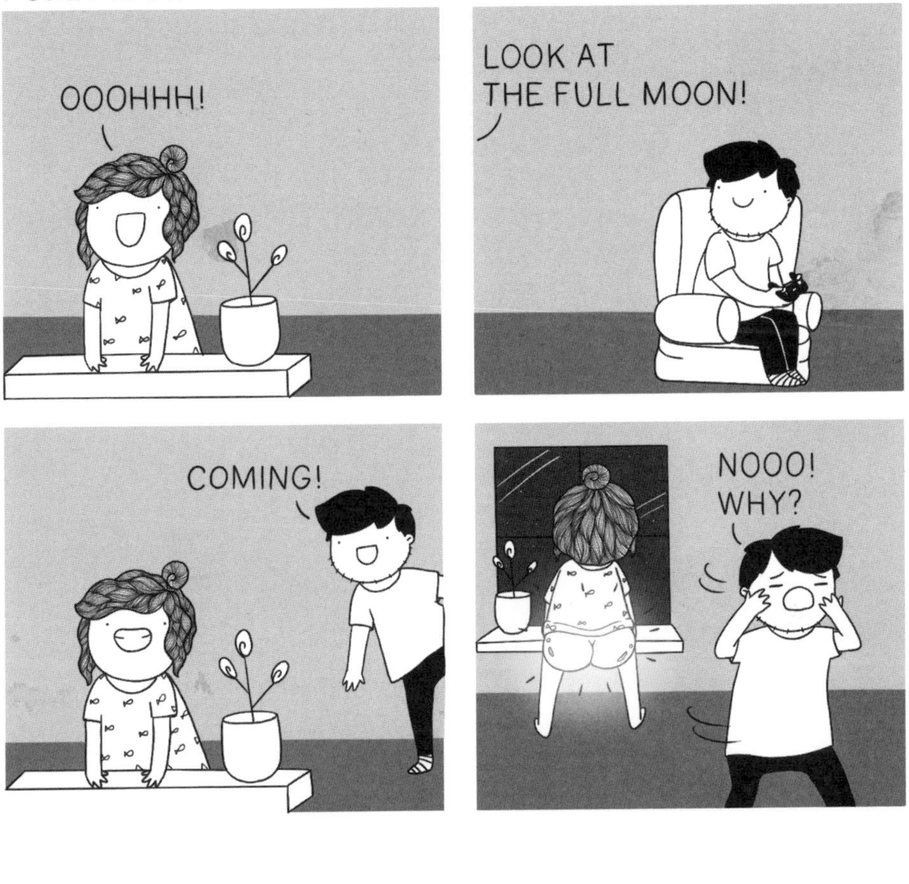
OOOHHH!
LOOK AT THE FULL MOON!
COMING!
NOOO! WHY?

THANKS BUDDY

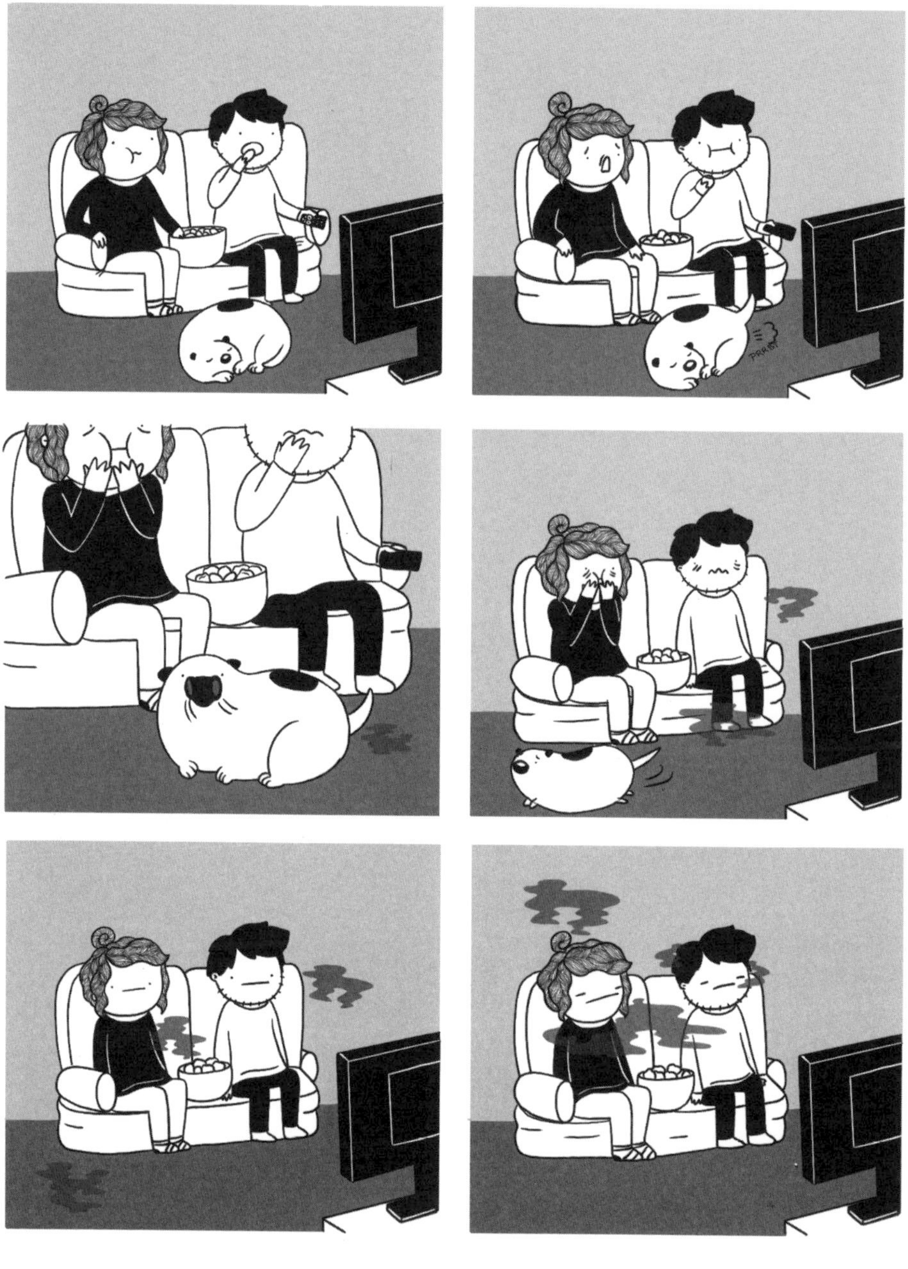
PRRBT

SHARE YOUR DREAMS

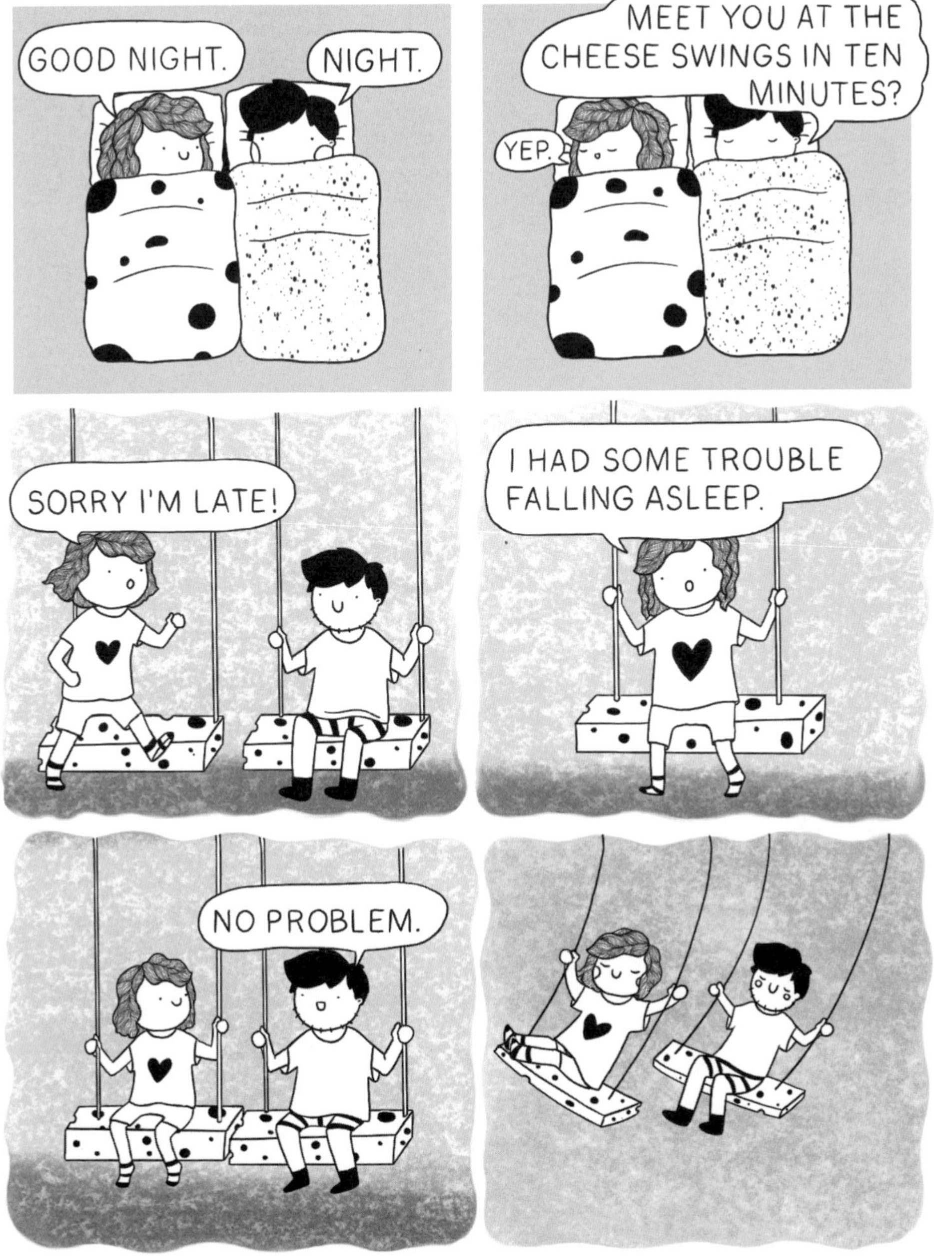
GOOD NIGHT.
NIGHT.
MEET YOU AT THE CHEESE SWINGS IN TEN MINUTES?
YEP.
SORRY I'M LATE!
I HAD SOME TROUBLE FALLING ASLEEP.
NO PROBLEM.

MARTYR

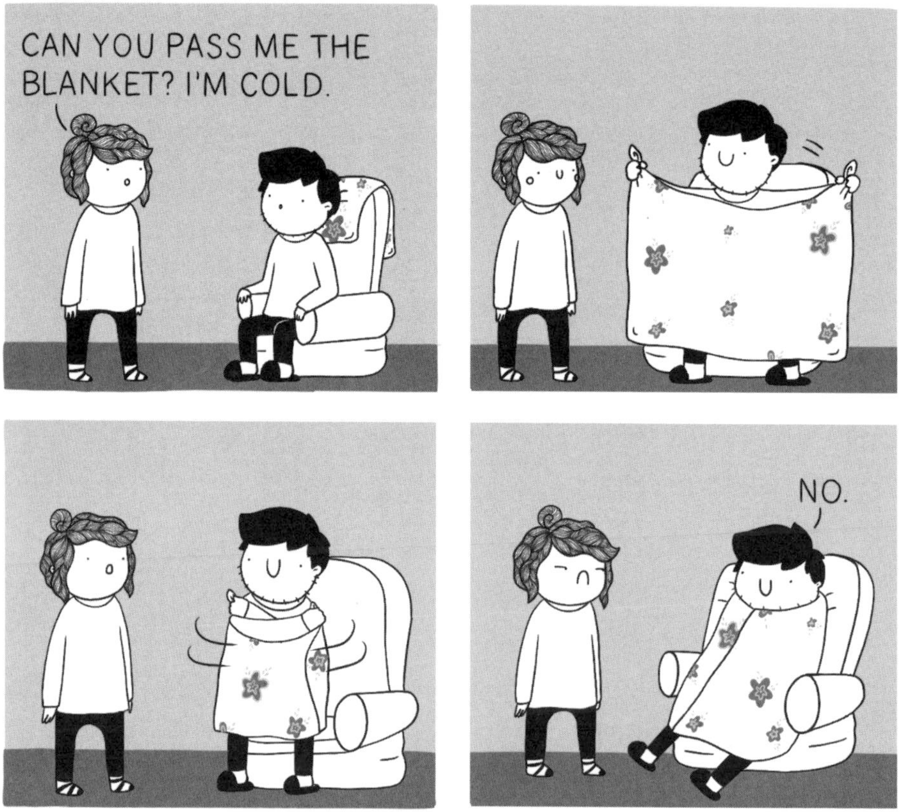
CAN YOU PASS ME THE BLANKET? I'M COLD.
NO.

NEVER-ENDING CIRCLE

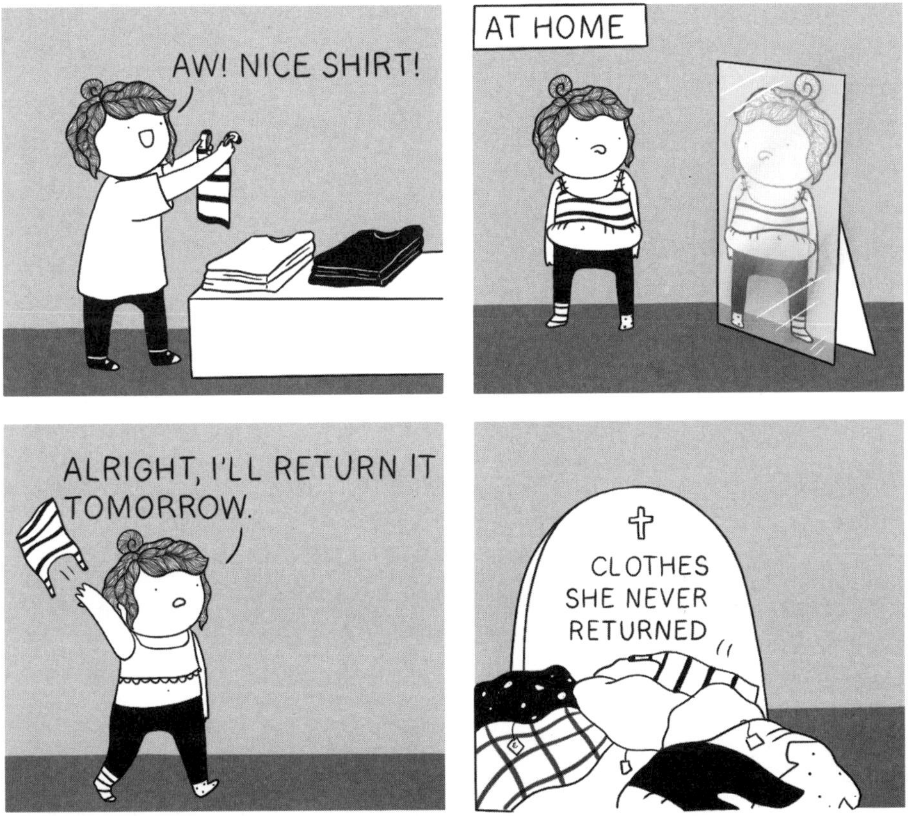
AW! NICE SHIRT!
AT HOME
ALRIGHT, I'LL RETURN IT TOMORROW.
CLOTHES SHE NEVER RETURNED

PEACEFUL NIGHT

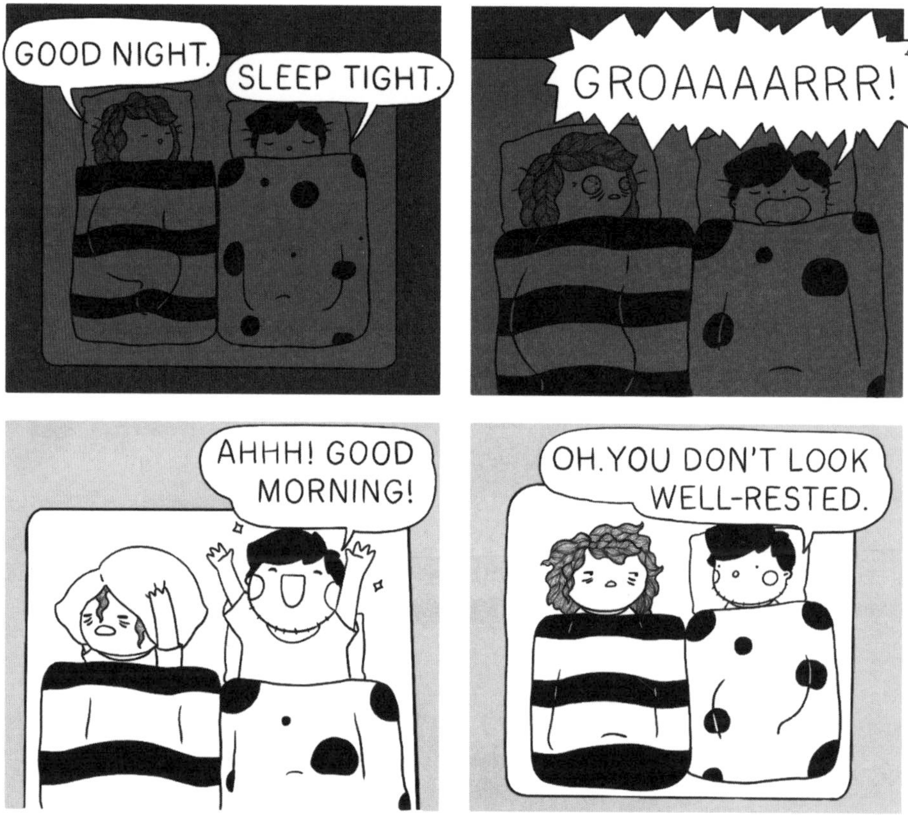
GOOD NIGHT.
SLEEP TIGHT.
GROAAAARRR!
AHHH! GOOD MORNING!
OH. YOU DON'T LOOK WELL-RESTED.

PERSISTENCE

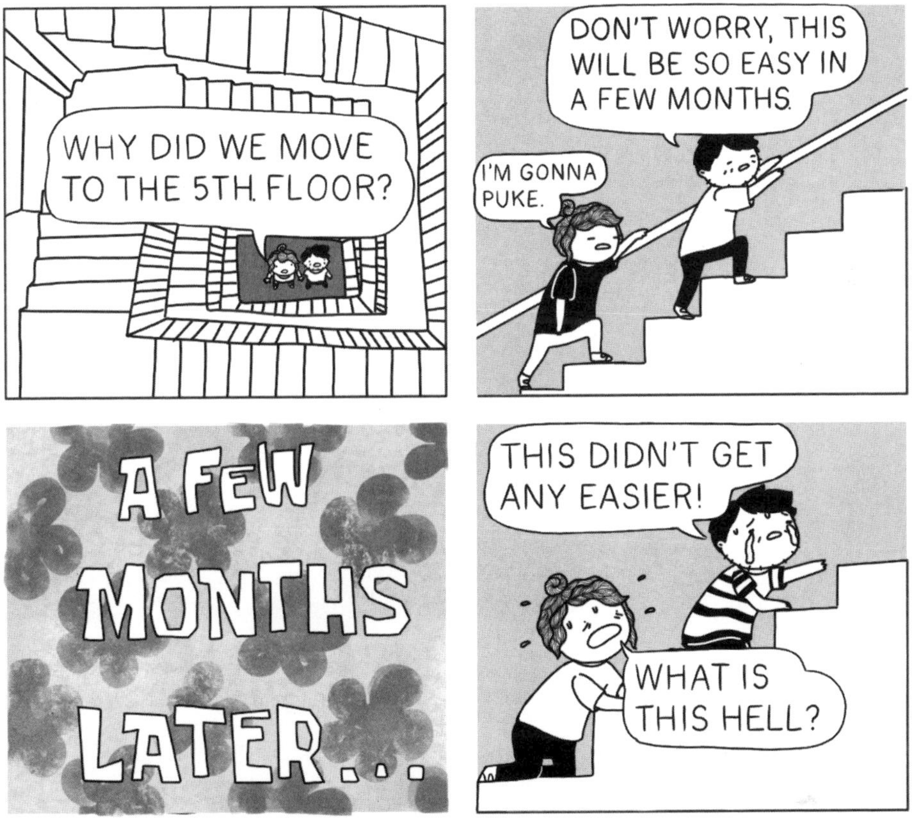

WHY DID WE MOVE TO THE 5TH FLOOR?
DON'T WORRY, THIS WILL BE SO EASY IN A FEW MONTHS.
I'M GONNA PUKE.
A FEW MONTHS LATER...
THIS DIDN'T GET ANY EASIER!
WHAT IS THIS HELL?

ROUTINE

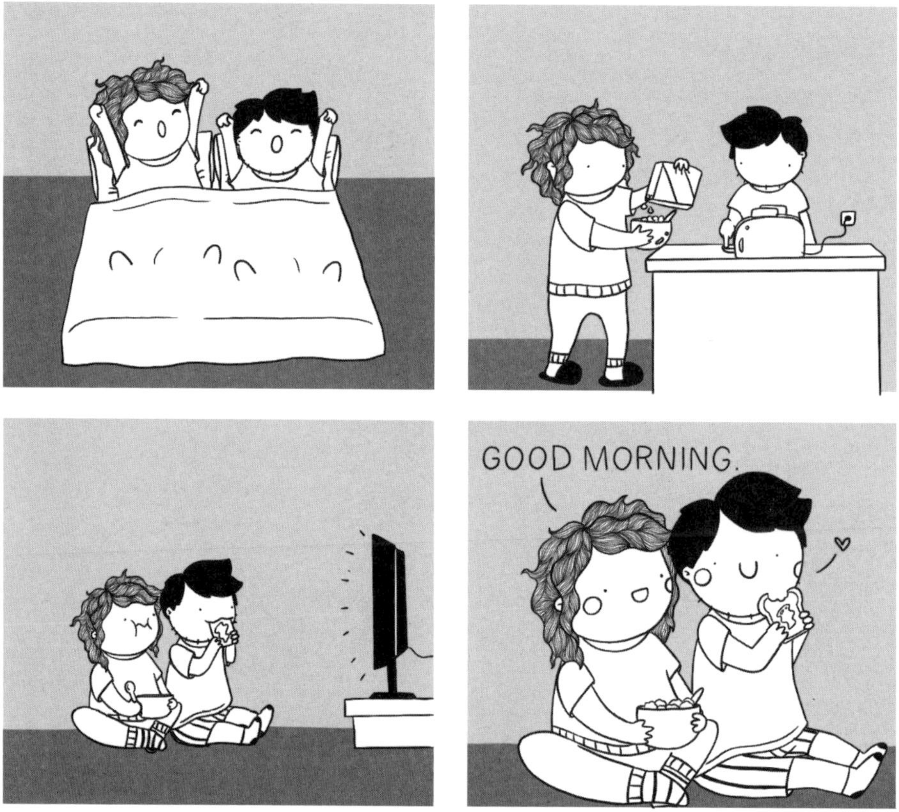
GOOD MORNING.

THE QUESTION

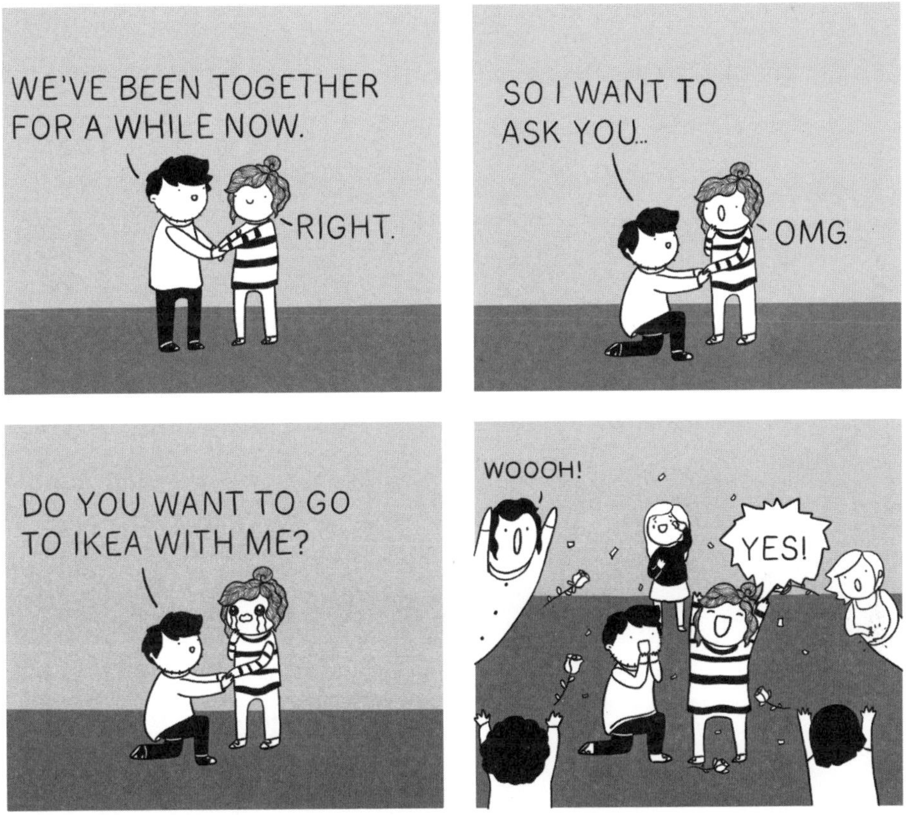
WE'VE BEEN TOGETHER FOR A WHILE NOW.
RIGHT.
SO I WANT TO ASK YOU...
OMG.
DO YOU WANT TO GO TO IKEA WITH ME?
WOOOH!
YES!

TREASURE HUNT

TOUCHY

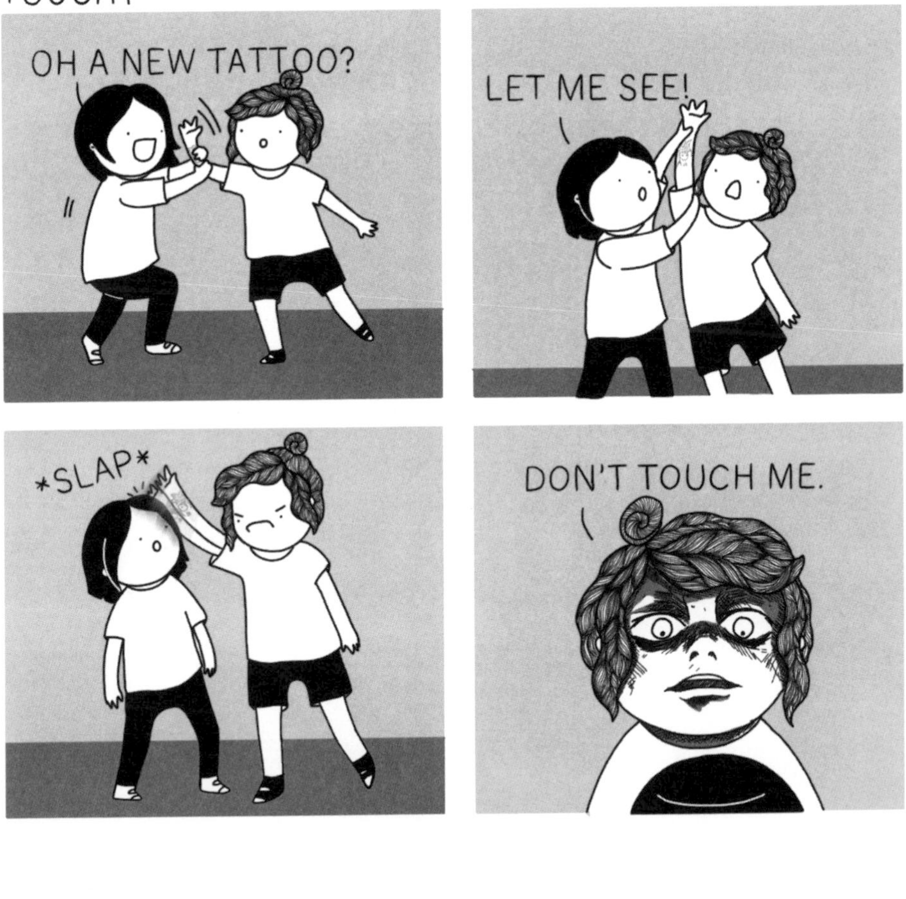
OH A NEW TATTOO?
LET ME SEE!
SLAP
DON'T TOUCH ME.

WHY?

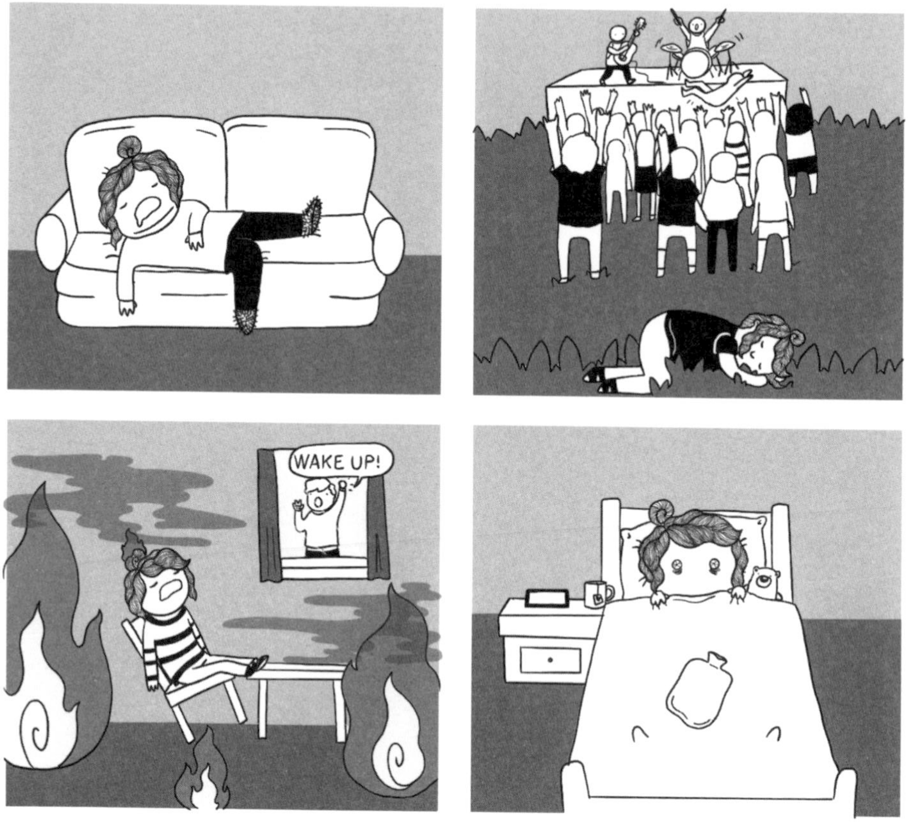
WAKE UP!

REFLEXES

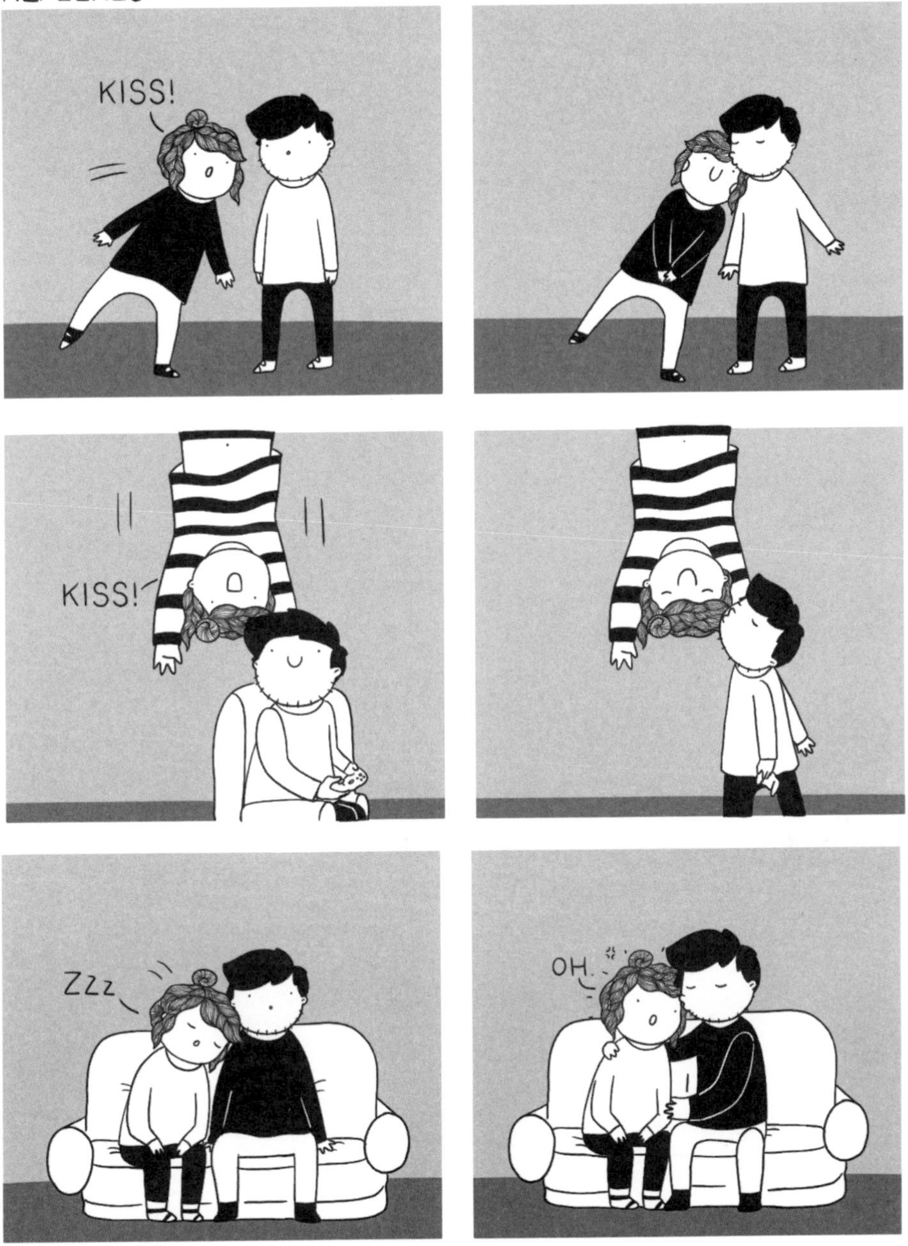
KISS!
KISS!
ZZz
OH.

THE LITTLE THINGS

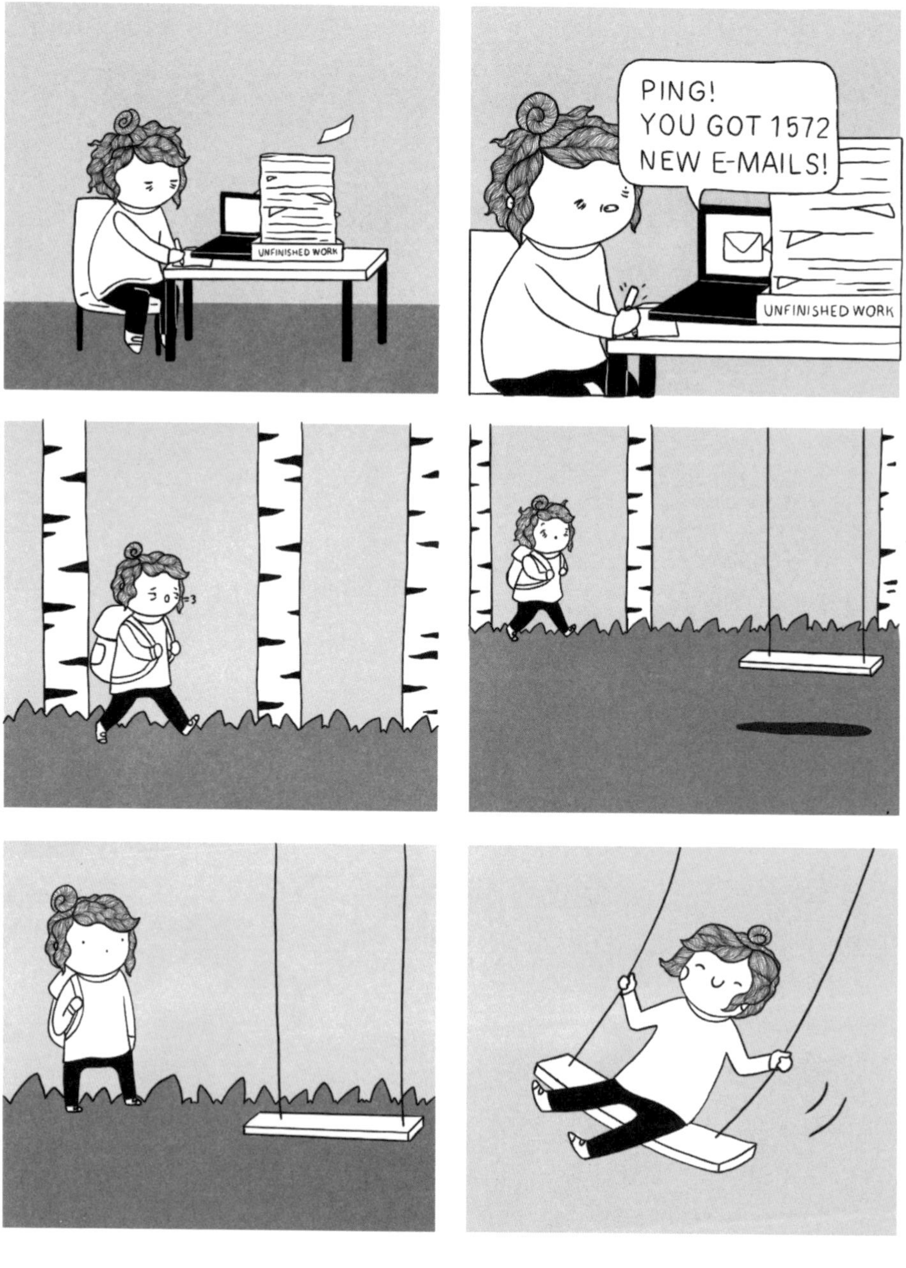
UNFINISHED WORK
PING! YOU GOT 1572 NEW E-MAILS!
UNFINISHED WORK

SPECIAL THANKS

To Elias,
Without you, there would be no Mrs. Frollein.

ABOUT THE AUTHOR

Mrs. Frollein is an ongoing webcomic about the life of its creator, Valérie Minelli. When she's not busy creating comics, Minelli loves to illustrate children's books and fangirl about whatever band she's currently into at the moment.